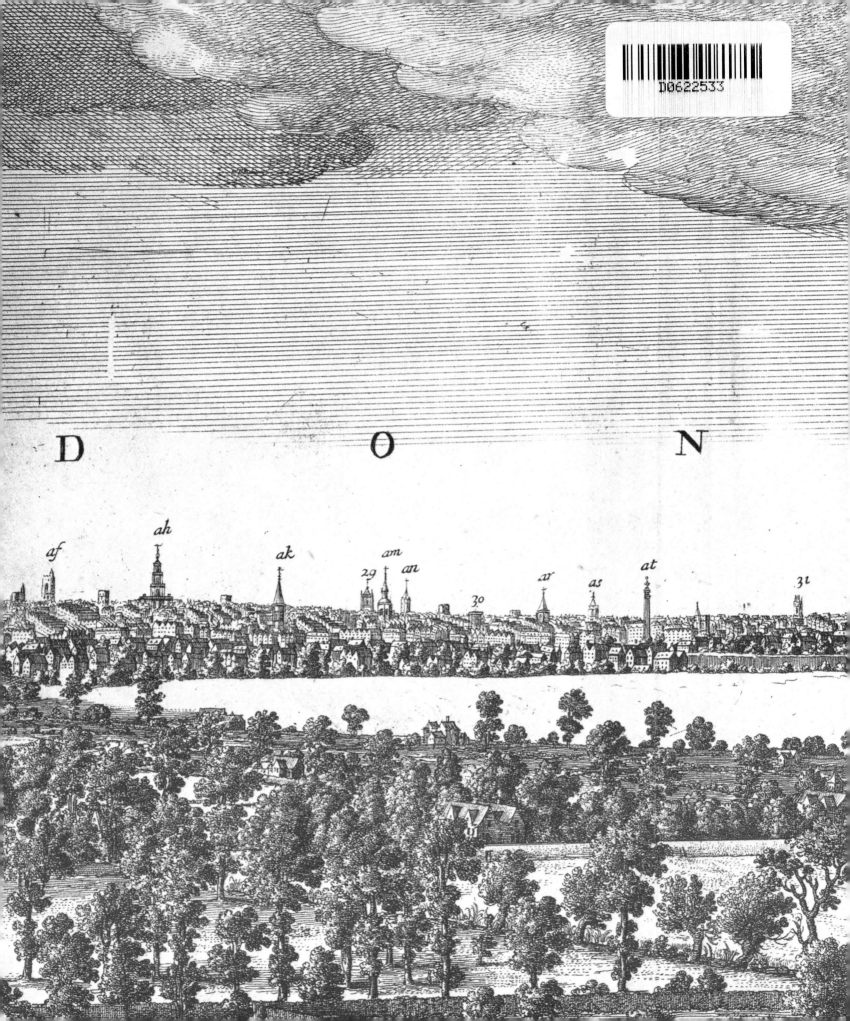

D O N

af ah ak am an 29 ar as at 30 31

THE CITY OF LONDON CHURCHES

THE CITY OF LONDON
CHURCHES

◆

A PICTORIAL REDISCOVERY

PHOTOGRAPHS BY DEREK KENDALL

Royal Commission on the
Historical Monuments of England

COLLINS & BROWN

First published in Great Britain in 1998 by Collins & Brown Limited
London House, Great Eastern Wharf, Parkgate Road, London SW11 4NQ

© Collins & Brown Limited 1998

Text and photographs © Crown copyright 1998. Published with the
permission of the Royal Commission on the Historical Monuments of
England on behalf of the Controller of HMSO.

10 8 6 4 2 1 3 5 7 9

British Library Cataloguing-in-Publication Data

A catalogue record for this book is available from the British Library

ISBN 1 85585 461 9 (hardback)
ISBN 1 85585 490 2 (paperback)

Designed by Toucan Books Limited, London
Designer: Bob Burroughs

Edited by Elizabeth Drury

Reproduction by Pixel Tech, Singapore

Printed and bound in Singapore

FRONT COVER: St Mary le Bow
BACK COVER (CLOCKWISE FROM TOP LEFT): All Hallows Barking by the
Tower, detail of font cover; St Anne and St Agnes, lectern and reredos;
The Spanish and Portuguese Synagogue, chandeliers; St Mary le Bow, nave.
TITLE PAGE: St Mary le Bow from St Mary Aldermary

CONTENTS

Foreword by Lord Faringdon,
Chairman of the Royal Commission on the Historical Monuments of England 6
Acknowledgements 7
Preface by the 132nd Bishop of London, the Right Reverend Richard Chartres 8
Introduction: The City Churches Recorded
by Peter Guillery 10

ALL HALLOWS BARKING BY THE TOWER	16	ST MARGARET PATTENS	140
ALL HALLOWS LONDON WALL	24	ST MARTIN LUDGATE	144
ST ANDREW HOLBORN	28	ST MARY ABCHURCH	150
ST ANDREW UNDERSHAFT	34	ST MARY ALDERMARY	156
ST ANDREW BY THE WARDROBE	38	ST MARY LE BOW	162
ST ANNE AND ST AGNES	42	ST MARY AT HILL	170
ST BARTHOLOMEW THE GREAT	48	ST MARY WOOLNOTH	174
ST BARTHOLOMEW THE LESS	56	ST MICHAEL CORNHILL	180
ST BENET PAUL'S WHARF	60	ST MICHAEL PATERNOSTER ROYAL	186
ST BOTOLPH WITHOUT ALDERSGATE	66	ST NICHOLAS COLE ABBEY	190
ST BOTOLPH ALDGATE	70	ST OLAVE HART STREET	194
ST BOTOLPH BISHOPSGATE	74	ST PETER CORNHILL	202
ST BRIDE FLEET STREET	80	ST SEPULCHRE WITHOUT NEWGATE	206
ST CLEMENT EASTCHEAP	88	ST STEPHEN WALBROOK	212
ST DUNSTAN IN THE WEST	90	ST VEDAST FOSTER LANE	216
ST EDMUND KING AND MARTYR	98	A CITYSCAPE OF TOWERS	220
ST ETHELBURGA BISHOPSGATE	102	THE CITY TEMPLE	222
ST GILES CRIPPLEGATE	104	THE DUTCH CHURCH AUSTIN FRIARS	224
ST HELEN BISHOPSGATE	110	JEWIN WELSH CHURCH	230
ST JAMES GARLICKHYTHE	116	ST ETHELDREDA ELY PLACE	232
ST KATHERINE CREE	120	ST MARY MOORFIELDS	236
ST LAWRENCE JEWRY	124	THE SPANISH AND PORTUGUESE SYNAGOGUE	240
ST MAGNUS THE MARTYR	128	THE TEMPLE CHURCH	244
ST MARGARET LOTHBURY	134		

Appendix: The Royal Commission on the Historical Monuments of England 252
Photographs Illustrated: RCHME Negative Numbers 253
Select Bibliography 254
Map and Information on Access to the City Churches 255
Index of Architects, Artists and Craftsmen 256

FOREWORD

BY THE RIGHT HONOURABLE LORD FARINGDON,
CHAIRMAN OF THE ROYAL COMMISSION ON THE HISTORICAL MONUMENTS OF ENGLAND

THIS BOOK PRESENTS a selection of photographs of the City Churches from a survey made by Derek Kendall, a senior photographer with the Royal Commission on the Historical Monuments of England. In publishing these photographs the Royal Commission aims to heighten awareness and improve understanding of the enduring glory of the City of London Churches.

The photographic survey covers all the parish churches and other buildings for worship in the City of London, except St Paul's Cathedral. Of the 39 Anglican buildings, 27 were recently subject to proposals considering closure or conversion. Terrorist bombs in 1992 and 1993 resulted in the almost total loss of St Ethelburga Bishopsgate, and damage to other churches. The need for up-to-date records of these buildings has been strongly underlined. The Royal Commission therefore undertook the first overall photographic survey of the churches since the 1920s, agreeing a programme and schedules in advance with English Heritage and the Corporation of London, the latter providing essential financial backing for the project.

During 1995 Derek Kendall photographed the 46 buildings externally and internally, in colour and black-and-white, using a large-format camera. The survey produced a total of over 2,000 photographs. It amounts to a narrative in 46 chapters — new, extensive, beautiful, different and highly evocative. It is also useful. The west lobby of St Magnus the Martyr (see page 128) was the site of a fire within months of the Royal Commission's photography. Our photographs were referred to in assessing the damage, a sad but timely substantiation of the practical value of the information.

In addition to the recent photographs, this book includes reminders of the existence of earlier records. A few early photographs have been included, all taken from the holdings of the National Monuments Record, the vast public archive of information on England's historic environment curated by the Royal Commission.

The survey and its publication here complement other important and positive recent initiatives relating to the City Churches. The future for the buildings is looking much rosier than it did five years ago. Let this book contribute therefore to what has become a celebration.

The Commissioners would like to thank all the Royal Commission staff involved in the survey and the publication of this book. In particular, we congratulate Derek Kendall on his achievement. Others who have made substantial contributions are Peter Guillery, who has written the text, Charlotte Bradbeer and June Warrington, who have assisted with both text and photographs, and Michael Seaforth and Tom Patterson, whose photographic printing was co-ordinated by Diane Kendall. Dr John Bold and Harriet Richardson have contributed to the editing of text.

Commissioners
Dr Peter Addyman MA (Cantab) FSA MIFA
Dr Malcolm Airs BA MA DPhil FSA
Ms Amanda Arrowsmith MA MBA
Professor Richard Bradley MA MIFA FSA
Professor Eric Fernie BA Hons CBE
Professor Michael Fulford PhD FSA
Dr Richard Gem MA FSA
Dr D. J. Keene MA FRHistS
Trevor Longman Esq BSc FBCS
Ms Helen Maclagan BA Hons
Dr Marilyn Palmer MA FSA
Miss Anne Riches FSA
Dr Wendy Sudbury MA (Cantab) DPhil
Mr Robert Yorke MA MSc

ACKNOWLEDGEMENTS

◆

Particular thanks are due to the Venerable George Cassidy, Archdeacon of London, and to all the incumbents, occupiers and wardens of the churches, too numerous to list, who have kindly helped with access and shared their intimate knowledge of the buildings.

The Royal Commission also wishes to express its gratitude to the Corporation of London for its professional and financial commitment to this project, without which it would not have come to fruition. We are particularly indebted to Ralph Hyde, Curator of Prints and Drawings in the Guildhall Library, and Annie Hampson, Assistant City Planning Officer.

The publishers of *The Buildings of England, Ireland, Scotland and Wales* very kindly allowed us to refer to pre-publication text for the latest edition of the City of London volume in that series. For this we are grateful to Bridget Cherry and Dr Simon Bradley.

Thanks also go to the following for advice and support that contributed to the survey and to this publication: Dr Roger Bowdler, English Heritage; Peter Cormack, William Morris Gallery; Stephen Croad, former Head of the National Monuments Record; Andrew Derrick, English Heritage; Donald Findlay, Council for the Care of Churches; Dr Gordon Higgott, English Heritage; Richard Pollard, Friends of the City Churches; Professor Andrew Saint, University of Cambridge; Dr John Schofield, Museum of London Archaeology Service; Teresa Sladen, architectural historian; Robert Thorne, Alan Baxter & Associates, consulting engineers.

An important impetus behind the decision to publish this book was a highly successful exhibition of a selection of the photographs in the crypt of St Paul's Cathedral in the autumn of 1996. In this connection thanks are due to Brigadier R. W. Acworth, Registrar at St Paul's, and to Trevor Cooper of the Ecclesiological Society, for arranging to extend the life of the exhibition at a conference on the City Churches.

PREFACE

---◆---

BY THE 132ND BISHOP OF LONDON, THE RIGHT REVEREND RICHARD CHARTRES

ONE WAG SUGGESTED RECENTLY that the City Churches faced three great threats, the Great Fire, the Luftwaffe and the Bishop of London in his various incarnations. It gave me particular pleasure therefore to have been invited to contribute this preface.

I am very glad that the publication of this handsome volume from the Royal Commission on the Historical Monuments of England illustrating the architectural riches of the churches of the City of London coincides with a recovery of confidence in the future of the churches as centres of imaginative Christian work in the Square Mile.

It used to be commonplace to describe the City Churches as a well-kept secret. Now the Diocese of London in conjunction with English Heritage and the City Corporation has commissioned and published a detailed survey of the Churches, while organizations such as the Friends of the City Churches and The Ecclesiological Society (of which I am proud to be a member) have stimulated a great deal of new interest with a programme of walks and conferences. This publication is part of the effort to open up the potential of London's ecclesiastical heritage to both citizens and visitors.

This is not merely a matter of treating the churches as an essay in the history of art but of using every means including the new interactive technology to present the Christian story in London so that tourists, if they wish, may recover the sense of pilgrimage.

At the same time a new chapter is opening in the tradition of using the City Churches as a base for important specialist work. Some parishes may have few residents, but their churches often serve as the anchorhold for worldwide networks. This is true, for example, of St Bride Fleet Street with its unique work among media professionals. This continues even though the head offices of the newspapers have moved further east into Docklands.

Another worldwide network that traces its origin to a City Church is The Samaritans, which exists to befriend those tempted to suicide. It was started by Prebendary Chad Varah in the crypt of St Stephen Walbrook.

Now the examples of such extended use are multiplying. The church of All Hallows London Wall has just been opened up again as a centre for a Christian Aid team, building bridges between the culture of the greatest financial centre in the world and the needs of the world's poorest. Still in progress are the developments at St Ethelburga, which suffered so grievously in the Bishopsgate bombing of 1993. An Oecumenical consortium is at work rebuilding the church to serve as a Centre for Reconciliation and Peace. Torn to pieces by sectarian violence, St Ethelburga will, I hope, be back at work in time for the Millennium, offering a creative addition to the City's range of international consultancies.

From the end of Roman times, the City of London has developed around Christian shrines. Churches, as the poet Philip Larkin suggested, are still able to robe our destinies in stone, and they continue to evoke strong emotions even among non attenders. The City Churches remain significant in the Christian missionary effort in London. Dilapidated buildings signal the decrepitude of faith with a terrible eloquence. The beauties of a church by Wren or Hawksmoor assert that there are other values in the world beyond price per square foot.

Any society that hopes to change creatively needs the strength that comes from anchorholds and continuities. If everything is in motion, then the result is mere frenzy. The churches remain while so much else has been swept away by the orgy of post-war development. With a cooperative effort between the Church, City institutions, conservation bodies, and above all the citizens of London, we can ensure that generations unborn will continue to enjoy what we have inherited and the rumour of God will continue to echo around the counting house.

+ Richard Londin:

The Bible from St Bartholomew the Great.

INTRODUCTION

◆

THE CITY CHURCHES RECORDED

BY PETER GUILLERY

LONDON'S CITY CHURCHES are acknowledged as one of the finest groups of ecclesiastical buildings in Europe. As a group they are firmly linked to Sir Christopher Wren, and rightly so. However, looked at individually, their interest is far, far wider. Among them are distinguished examples of virtually every major phase of English architectural history, all within the Square Mile that is the City of London, the historic core of the much bigger city.

Roman and Saxon remains can be found at All Hallows Barking by the Tower and St Bride Fleet Street. Though fragmentary, these are reminders of London's antiquity; indeed, St Paul's Cathedral was founded in 604 and has presided over the City Churches ever since. The *c*.1090 crypt at St Mary le Bow, and St Bartholomew the Great, founded as an Augustinian priory church in 1123, are much more substantial early survivals, exceptional in London as powerfully evocative works of Romanesque architecture. They are also evidence of the status of the Church in medieval society, the former in connection with the Archbishop of Canterbury's Court of Arches, the latter as a great monastic church.

By the end of the 12th century London had grown to have more than 100 parish churches and 13 monastic houses. Little of this survives. The Temple Church is an important exception. The Gothic style is said to have been introduced to London in its circular nave, consecrated in 1185; its chancel of 50 years later is more refined Gothic architecture. St Helen Bishopsgate has an unusual twin-nave arrangement reflecting the addition around 1210 of a Benedictine nunnery church alongside an earlier parish church.

From the later medieval period the *c*.1390 south arcade of St Ethelburga still stands, and St Olave Hart Street and St Sepulchre without Newgate still have substantial amounts of mid 15th-century fabric. Both the latter churches retain what had by that time become the standard form of a nave and two aisles. From around the time of the English Reformation come the stately Perpendicular rebuildings of St Andrew Undershaft of 1520-32 and St Giles Cripplegate of *c*.1550. The City was well endowed with churches, so the transition from medieval to modern during the first century after the Reformation took place with little more new church building, though much attention was given to the internal layout of churches because of changing liturgical requirements. An exception is St Katherine Cree of 1628-31, which juxtaposes Gothic and classical features in a manner that tells us much about architecture in this turbulent period.

The Great Fire of 1666 devastated the City of London, destroying or badly damaging 87 of its 108 churches. The population of the City had already begun to decline, as outlying districts grew. By 1670 agreement had been reached that 51 of the destroyed or damaged churches would be rebuilt. Parliament appointed a Commission, comprising the Archbishop of Canterbury, the Bishop of London, and the Lord Mayor of the City of London, to oversee a rebuilding programme funded by a tax on coal brought into the City. The King's Surveyor General, Dr (later Sir) Christopher Wren, was appointed to direct the programme. He had assistance from Robert Hooke and Edward Woodroffe, later succeeded by John Oliver, Nicholas Hawksmoor and William Dickinson. These men oversaw building contracts carried out by a range of masons, bricklayers, carpenters and other craftsmen.

Recent scholarship has sought to identify the separate responsibilities of the members of Wren's team. In particular, it has become clear that Robert Hooke had extensive design responsibilities from the outset. Even so, Wren was in charge, and the most architecturally adventurous church designs were certainly his. The 51 churches were finally completed in 1716; of these 23 survive. Wren was also responsible for the concurrent rebuilding of St Paul's Cathedral, the vast classical edifice that stands above and amid these churches. Building work on the cathedral carried on from 1675 through to 1710.

The 'Wren' churches exhibit astonishing variety and invention. Wren and Hooke were both scientists before they were architects; in their church building work they were above all empirical. They dealt ingeniously with the constrained sites and partial survival of medieval fabric that remained despite the Fire. Indeed medieval plans were often retained, as they had been in rebuildings begun before the Commission was set up, at St Sepulchre without Newgate (1667-71) and St Michael Cornhill (1669-72). Most remarkably in this context, St Mary Aldermary (1679-82) demonstrates the survival of the Gothic style under Wren.

Nonetheless, the City Church rebuildings were the first major opportunity to address the liturgical requirements of the Church of England in new buildings designed in a classical style, a process for which there were good Continental parallels. To use Wren's words, there was a need for spaces 'fitted to be auditories', that is, interiors where the congregation could 'hear distinctly, and see the Preacher'. This meant departing from the traditional form of pre-Reformation churches, a processional nave and aisles with subsidiary chapels. Buildings with centralized plans were introduced. The cross-in-square plan, perhaps influenced by Dutch precedent, and more subtle auditory plans combining a more traditional longitudinal emphasis with centrality, possibly related to earlier 17th-century buildings in outlying parts of London, were adopted at St Mary at Hill (1670-4), St James Garlickhythe (1676-84), St Anne and St Agnes (1677-80), St Martin Ludgate (1677-86), and, perhaps, St Magnus the Martyr (1668-84). Galleries were an important means of providing adequate seating close to the heart of such churches.

Wren in particular had a remarkable ability to create internal grandeur within small spaces, through a variety of devices. This is most excitingly evident in two domed churches, St Stephen Walbrook (1672-80) and St Mary Abchurch (1681-6). In contrast to the classical richness of these interiors are the simple red-brick and box-like 'Dutch' exteriors, best exemplified by the charming St Benet Paul's Wharf (1678-84).

And, of course, there are the spires, cheerfully diverse. Wren's St Mary le Bow (1668-80) set the standard, but many were completed only in the later stages of the rebuilding programme. A number of the most inventive later spires, including St Bride Fleet Street (1701-3) and St Vedast Foster Lane (1709-12), have recently been reattributed to the young Nicholas Hawksmoor, who was exploring the possibilities of Baroque plasticity more successfully than any other English architect. The idiosyncratic St Mary Woolnoth of 1716-27, entirely by Hawksmoor, is a characteristically sophisticated manifestation of this architect's mature Baroque style.

It is generally acknowledged that the City Churches collectively contain one of the most important ensembles of fully documented decorative carved wood fittings anywhere in England, indeed in Europe. Fitting out the churches, with pews (including galleries), a communion table (with or without rails) and a reredos (altarpiece), a pulpit with a tester (sounding board) and a font, was the responsibility of each parish, and it involved numerous skilled joiners and other craftsmen.[1] At St Mary Abchurch there is a reredos that is exceptional in that it is documented as being by Grinling Gibbons, the period's most renowned woodcarver. Other particularly fine interiors in respect of their fittings are at St Benet Paul's Wharf, St Martin Ludgate, and St Margaret Lothbury. In a different tradition, but as exquisitely furnished and beautifully preserved, is the Spanish and Portuguese Synagogue of 1699-1701.

Funerary monuments are legion. Particularly impressive groupings can be seen at St Olave Hart Street, St Dunstan in the West, St Helen Bishopsgate, St Bartholomew the Great and All Hallows Barking by the Tower. A speciality of the City is its large collection of attractive sword-rests, for use by the Lord Mayor's swordbearer. Other common fittings include organs, chandeliers, Royal Arms and poor boxes.

A number of the churches that had survived the Great Fire needed to be rebuilt in the 18th century. Into this category fall the 'three Botolphs', solid Georgian churches: St Botolph Bishopsgate, of 1725-8 by James Gould, St Botolph Aldgate, of 1741-4 by George Dance the Elder, and St Botolph without Aldersgate, of 1789-91 by Nathaniel Wright. All Hallows London Wall of 1765-7 was designed by George Dance the Younger when he was only 24, in a precociously refined Neoclassical style. Early 19th-century eclecticism is represented by the pre-Revival Gothic of St Bartholomew the Less, of 1823-5 by Thomas Hardwick, and St Dunstan in the West, of 1830-3 by John Shaw, both, unusually, with octagonal plans.

In the Victorian period there was, to a greater or lesser degree, intervention everywhere. A number of churches were demolished (see below), and many restorations were largely negative in their effect; 17th-century classicism was then widely unpopular. However, some work was exemplary in character. William Gibbs Rogers's superb woodwork, as at St Mary at Hill in 1848-9, is all-but indistinguishable from that of the Wren period. Sir George Gilbert Scott's restoration of St Michael Cornhill in 1857-60, in an Early Christian style, was an intelligent adaptation of a classical building to a style more acceptable to the High Anglican demands of the day. A generation later John Francis Bentley's redecoration of St Botolph Aldgate in 1888-91 included a marvellously distinctive Arts and Crafts plasterwork ceiling. St Bartholomew the Great was sensitively restored by Sir Aston Webb, in phases, from 1886 to 1898. There is little early stained glass in the City Churches, but there is still a good amount from the 19th century, including the notable windows of 1858 at St Michael Cornhill, by Clayton and Bell, and the 1875-6 east window at St Andrew Undershaft, by Heaton, Butler and Bayne.

In 1940-1 air raids devastated London, with further war damage occurring up to 1944. Famously, St Paul's Cathedral survived (Fig. 1), but 21 of the remaining 47 parish churches were reduced to ruins. Thirteen of the damaged City Churches were rebuilt in the 1950s and 1960s, decades which the heritage-minded 1990s tend to regard as the Dark Ages in terms of dealing with historic buildings. Yet much of what was done then was 'in keeping', but unslavishly and sometimes unselfconsciously so. We do not readily recognize the degree to which the fabric of the City Churches is less than 50 years old.

Commitment to continuing traditions of architecture and craftsmanship, classical and Gothic, as well as to the introduction of Modernism, was expressed in varying manners, with results that are now beginning to be judged with detachment 30 to 40 years later. On the whole, the imaginative conservatism of the post-war rebuildings has aged

---

[1] These craftsmen are not named here, for want of space. They are well documented elsewhere: S. Bradley and N. Pevsner, *The Buildings of England: London 1: The City of London* (London, 1997), and P. Jeffery, *The City Churches of Sir Christopher Wren* (London, 1996).

well. St Vedast Foster Lane, of 1953-63 by Stephen Dykes Bower, was rearranged as a serene collegiate chapel, with opposed seating, and stained glass by Brian Thomas, whose excellent work is also visible at St Sepulchre without Newgate and St Andrew Holborn. St Bride Fleet Street, of 1955-7, was similarly re-ordered by Godfrey Allen, and lavishly reinvented as an impressive space. All Hallows Barking by the Tower, of 1948-58 by Seely and Paget, was creatively reconstructed with exposed concrete components. St Mary le Bow, of 1954-64 by Lawrence King, reproduced Wren's essential architecture, but made few other concessions to tradition — either liturgical or architectural — incorporating stylized glass by John Hayward, who also contributed windows to St Michael Paternoster Royal. High-quality woodwork of traditional form but widely differing character was put into St Lawrence Jewry, 1954-7 by Cecil Brown, and St Andrew by the Wardrobe, 1959-61 by Marshall Sisson. The Dutch Church Austin Friars was completely rebuilt in 1950-4 to designs by Arthur Bailey, its harmonious interior reflecting some of the best qualities of 1950s architecture. A footnote to this period is the dismantling and re-erection in Fulton, Missouri, USA, of St Mary Aldermanbury in 1965-6.

History does not stop. St Stephen Walbrook was controversially re-ordered in 1978-87, with the introduction of an altarpiece by Henry Moore. Then, in April 1992 and April 1993, IRA bombs damaged several City Churches, the second bomb largely destroying St Ethelburga. Arising from this damage, St Helen Bishopsgate was restored and substantially re-ordered in 1995, to designs by Quinlan Terry in a scheme that was strongly opposed by many conservationists.

Recording the Churches

The history of the City Churches in the 20th century, as indeed in every century, is testament to the mutability of fabric, and thereby to the value of recording. The documentation of buildings depends on pictorial representation and, in these terms, architectural photography is information. The practical aims of recording, the provision of information for present and future understanding, govern the work of the Royal Commission on the Historical Monuments of England. However, there are more fundamental purposes to architectural records, sometimes overlooked in the rush to classify information as useful. Great buildings are sources of pleasure. Records can provide access to this pleasure. Enjoyment is perhaps even more basic than information as a starting point for understanding.

The recording of the City Churches has a long history. These buildings are certainly among the most documented of England's historic monuments. This should not lead to the complacent conclusion that we know enough. Recording reflects changing perceptions of what constitutes historic interest and what might be an appropriate approach to documenting that interest. Any record is a subjective, partial and provisional statement, and every age sees the past in a different way.

The beginning of purposeful recording of the City Churches can be said to be John Stow's *Survey of London*, first published in 1598. Detailed accounts of churches were included in what was effectively the first antiquarian and topographical description of contemporary London. Partially motivated by discontent with the pace and character of development in the burgeoning Elizabethan city, Stow looked at London as a changing place with its own history. Where Stow had begun, others followed in the 18th century. Even before the Wren churches had all acquired their spires Edward Hatton was describing them, and, soon after, John Strype prepared a new edition of Stow's *Survey* that encompassed the rebuilt City.[2] The celebration of Wren's achievement was boosted by his own family,[3] while other antiquarianism looked beyond the recent past, recording the churches that had escaped the Great Fire.[4]

By the beginning of the 19th century Wren's City Churches were recognized by an informed elite as being a highpoint in English architectural history. Architects referred to them as exemplars, and they were described and drawn in topographical studies.[5] Topographical survey tends to arise from or foster catholic tastes, but many writers in this period saw no need to be self-effacing; opinionated polemic remained at the heart of such recording, and criticism was both architectural and liturgical.

Since the 1830s the history of the City Churches has been a story of peril and rescue, threat and reprieve. During the 19th century declining population and church attendance in the City intersected with growing appreciation of the buildings. Recording acquired a position at the fulcrum of the demolition/preservation see-saw. It has been both a hedge against loss, a minimum position in the event of demolition, and a means of preventing that demolition.

In 1856 the City of London had 74 churches serving a resident population of 54,000. As Dickens observed, 'There are few more striking indications of the changes of manners and customs that two or three hundred years had brought about, than these deserted churches . . . They remain like the tombs of the old citizens who lie beneath them and around them, monuments of another age.'[6] Charles Blomfield, Bishop of

[2] E. Hatton, *A New View of London* (2 vols, London, 1708); J. Strype, *A Survey of the Cities of London and Westminster . . . by John Stow* (London, 1720).

[3] C. Wren, *Parentalia: Memoirs of the Family of the Wrens*, ed. S. Wren (London, 1750).

[4] R. West and W. H. Toms, *Perspective views of all the ancient churches and other buildings in the cities of London and Westminster* (London, 1736-9).

[5] For example, J. P. Malcolm, *Londinium Redivivum* (4 vols, London, 1803-7), and G. Godwin and J. Britton, *The Churches of London*, 2 vols (London, 1838).

[6] C. Dickens, *The Uncommercial Traveller* (London, 1861).

London, had rejected a plan of 1833 to demolish 13 churches, only to work later on a scheme that would have demolished 29. His successor, Bishop Tait, achieved the Union of Benefices Act of 1860, which set in train what we would now term 'rationalization', leading to the demolition of 16 City Churches between 1867 and 1900. Twelve of Wren's buildings, including some of his best, were in this group (Fig. 2).

Many fittings were rescued and dispersed to new homes, some of them in other City Churches, as in Walter Tapper's magnificent 1890s refurnishing of St Margaret Lothbury. There was strong opposition to the demolitions, and appreciation of the City Churches could be passionate: 'St Paul's bereft of its surrounding steeples, is to us as a parent bereft of her children . . . I desire their preservation, because in a future generation, when the battle of the styles has been fought, and the people are catholic in thought and taste, I can well imagine how much they may be appreciated and praised of all.'[7] Some of the buildings were photographed prior to demolition, but not systematically. Among the most precious early photographs of the City Churches are street scenes taken for purposes other than formal building recording. Other photographs were published to provide 'reliable illustrations of what we have but may yet lose'.[8]

Pressure to reduce the number of churches in the City continued, with Church Commissions proposing up to 19 more demolitions in 1899 and 1919. Opposition to these schemes, largely on architectural grounds, was effective, though gradually six more churches were demolished in the period up to 1939. During this time the recording of the

1. St Paul's Cathedral in the Blitz.

buildings became institutionalized, growing more thorough and archaeological as the protection of historic monuments gained recognition as a function of the State. The Royal Commission on the Historical Monuments of England (RCHME) was established in 1908 to 'make an inventory of the Ancient and Historical Monuments and Constructions connected with or illustrative of the contemporary culture, civilisation and conditions of life of the people in England . . . from the earliest times to the year 1700'. This placed the Wren churches at the end of history (later revised to 1714, and subsequently altogether disavowed); they were also at the apogee of conventional architectural taste.

During the 1920s the Royal Commission recorded the City

[7] A. H. Mackmurdo, *Wren's City Churches* (Orpington, 1883).
[8] G. H. Birch, *London Churches of the 17th and 18th Centuries* (London, 1896).

2. St Anthonin Budge Row, one of Wren's finest small churches (demolished 1874), as depicted on a tablet in St Mary Aldermary.

A remarkable individual contribution to the documentation of the City Churches at this time was made by Gerald Cobb, whose work was both scholarly and personal.[13] He compiled albums of photographs, engravings and cuttings, many of which were deposited in the NBR, which was amalgamated with the Royal Commission in 1963. Among distinguished architectural photographers who recorded the City Churches in the post-war period were Gordon Barnes and A. F. Kersting, both of whose work can also be seen in the NBR. Professor William Grimes's excavations at St Bride Fleet Street in 1952 took place at the beginning of the application of archaeology to standing churches.

The City's population was still decreasing after the war, yet a consensus had been established that no more City Churches should be demolished. The City of London (Guild Churches) Act of 1952 addressed this by creating a unique category of church, with a status between that of a parish church in use and a formally redundant church. The 1971 Buckley Commission argued against further demolitions, but suggested redundancy and alternative use for nine churches, proposals that were successfully opposed.

With the rising strength of the conservation movement in the 1970s there came a growing concern for the setting of the churches.[14] The scale of new buildings was obliterating the City's spire-scape. John Betjeman wrote, 'As the noise and reek of diesel oil in the streets grow greater, and as the impersonal slabs of cellular offices rise higher into the sky, so do the churches which remain in the City of London today become more valuable to us. They maintain a human scale and still mark off the City from the rest of London, recalling lost lanes of little shops where clerks could spend their lunch hour. The City churches also reflect by their variety, the varied quality of the City itself.'[15] This still rings true — perhaps, after all, nostalgia is what it used to be. The value of the churches as surviving small-scale buildings has grown greater, as the pace of regenerative change has intensified.

With the buildings apparently safe from demolition the purpose of recording has been reconsidered. An archaeological

Churches, preparing meticulously detailed descriptions of early architectural features and fittings, carefully measured and phased plans, and photographs.[9] In parallel, the Survey of London, established in 1894 and subsequently taken under the wing of the London County Council (then absorbed by the Royal Commission in 1986), prepared substantial monographs on St Helen Bishopsgate, All Hallows Barking, and St Bride Fleet Street.[10] Private initiatives reinforced and enhanced these official recording programmes, with the Wren Society publishing volumes reproducing drawings, old prints and photographs of the City Churches.[11]

The National Buildings Record (NBR) was founded in 1940 as a direct result of air raids, to make photographic and other records of historic buildings in danger of destruction.[12]

[9] Royal Commission on Historical Monuments, *London*, iv, *The City* (London, 1929).

[10] *The Survey of London*, ix, *The Church of St. Helen, Bishopsgate* (London, 1924); *The Survey of London*, xii, *The Church of All Hallows, Barking* (London, 1929 and 1934); *The Survey of London*, xv, *The Parish of All Hallows, Barking* (London, 1934); *The Survey of London*, monograph 15, *The Church of St. Bride, Fleet Street* (London, 1944).

[11] The Wren Society, ix-x (Oxford, 1932-3).

[12] Some such recording was published, as in J. M. Richards ed., *The Bombed Buildings of Britain* (London, 1947) and C. H. Holden and W. G. Holford, *The City of London: A Record of Destruction and Survival* (London, 1951).

[13] G. Cobb, *The Old Churches of London* (3 edns, London 1941-8), revised as *London City Churches* (London, 1977).

[14] P. Burman, *Save the City* (London, 1976).

[15] J. Betjeman, *The City of London Churches* (London, 1974).

approach has gained in importance, while the Royal Commission's programmes have provision for 'emergency recording'. This work covers many eventualities, among which is disaster response. A serious fire at St Mary at Hill in 1988 (page 172) and an accident at St James Garlickhythe in 1991 (page 116) prompted photographic recording. The bombs of 1992 and 1993 were more devastating, and extensive recording by various parties followed.

In the meantime the future of the City Churches in relation to the Church of England's pastoral responsibilities was again being considered. Bishop Hope established the City Churches Commission in 1992, to which in 1994 the Templeman Report proposed that there should be 27 'reserve churches', for which demolition was 'unthinkable', but for which closure, redundancy, and conversion to other use were to be considered.

These developments prompted vigorous debate, as in the 1860s and 1920s, and provided the backcloth to the survey published here, as well as to other initiatives. Despite all the recording that had gone before it was clear in 1994 that there was a need for new work. No overall survey of the City Churches had been carried out since the 1920s. Since then many of the buildings had been substantially renewed. Furthermore, there was very little publicly held colour photography. Accordingly the Royal Commission's photographic survey was planned with the Corporation of London and English Heritage.

In parallel, the Diocese of London, English Heritage and the Corporation of London joined to commission Alan Baxter and Associates, consulting engineers, to make a survey of the history, condition and use of the buildings, which was carried out in 1995. Other new publications included a review of knowledge relating to the Saxon and Medieval City Churches, covering valuable recent archaeological recording at several churches, largely those that had suffered damage, and a comprehensive architectural history of the Wren churches.[16] At the same time the Friends of the City Churches was formed to act as a focus for interest and, in 1996, the Ecclesiological Society mounted a conference, 'The City Churches: their history and future'. From Bishop Chartres there has emerged renewed commitment to the churches remaining open as functioning parts of the Church. A City Churches Development Group was set up in 1997.

It will be clear that any attempt at a definitive photographic survey would have been hubristic folly. Derek Kendall's photography is one account of a subject of which many others have been rendered, and as such part of the Royal Commission's duty to provide a continuing remembrance of the human landscape. In the context of other initiatives and the existence of historic holdings, it was considered appropriate to take an informed but subjective approach to the photography. In a sense this survey is a successor to the Royal Commission's very different work of the 1920s, with its measured drawings and detailed texts. These methods remain at the heart of the Royal Commission's practice, and in many other situations are our most useful tools. However, information about buildings can be usefully presented in many ways.

The survey covers all buildings for worship in the City, excluding St Paul's Cathedral. Its core is the 39 surviving current or former Anglican parish churches. For topographical thoroughness the City's handful of buildings erected for other religious worship is included, along with a Roman Catholic church, St Etheldreda, Ely Place, that is strictly just beyond the City boundary. Thus 46 buildings are recorded, producing a corpus of over 2,000 photographs. Isolated church towers and chapels within buildings erected for other purposes are not covered.

The approach to the photography was comprehensive and inclusive, agreed in advance through consultation with experts, but not exhaustive. Many little-known features and spaces, such as vestries, crypts and belfries, were brought to light. In selecting images for publication some traditional views and well-known features have been omitted, and some typical or unregarded features have been included, to embrace the obscure, the incidental, the humorous, the sad and, not least, the sacred. The buildings are valuable to those of all faiths and of none. As architecture, or Ark, each is a repository of great human achievement. As a group they are particularly precious since they stand in a place where the monolithic imperatives of an international financial centre tend to obscure both the beauty and the dirt of earthly reality. London is one of the world's greatest cities, and its continuing vitality depends on change and regeneration. Yet it is perhaps significant that as working patterns and attitudes to urban life change the decline in the City's resident population is at last being reversed.

Through Derek Kendall's photographs, a group of historic monuments that has been repeatedly assessed takes on new life. Literally defined, a monument is that which reminds. Indeed, Wren's epitaph in St Paul's Cathedral tells us '*si monumentum requiris, circumspice*' (if you seek his monument, look around you). The word monument is here conventionally linked to the surviving, the solid and the durable, but, if we really do look around, its potency can be linked to the fleeting, the quotidian and the unexceptional.

Architectural photography bridges the gap between the permanent and the transient. It is at once wholly empirical and wholly subjective. A record is an interpretation; it is not virtual reality, neither a substitute for a building nor an alternative to preservation. In that spirit these photographs are a 1990s celebration of the glory that is the City Churches.

---

[16] J. Schofield *et al*, 'Saxon and Medieval Parish Churches in the City of London: A Review', in *Transactions of the London and Middlesex Archaeological Society*, xlv (London, 1994), pp. 23-145; P. Jeffery, *op. cit.*

ALL HALLOWS BARKING BY THE TOWER

ALL HALLOWS, close to the Tower of London, was formerly a possession of the Abbey of Barking. The church is unique in London in retaining a section of its Anglo-Saxon walls, and much 15th-century fabric also survives. The ignition of gunpowder in Tower Street in 1658 caused damage to the church, and it was from the newly rebuilt west tower that Samuel Pepys surveyed the Great Fire in 1666, 'the saddest sight of desolation that I ever saw'. In 1940 a second explosion, caused by incendiary bombs, gutted the building. A sweeping and imaginative reconstruction in a Perpendicular Gothic style was carried out by Lord Mottistone, the lead partner of Seely and Paget, in 1948-58. Among the interesting monuments are some that relate to Toc H, a society founded by a rector of All Hallows, P. B. 'Tubby' Clayton, to perpetuate the comradeship of the 1914-18 war.

The fittings in All Hallows are a mixture of original, post-war and resited items, some of the earlier ones being of particularly high quality. The oak litany desk (above) is a remnant of a Jacobean pulpit; the limewood font cover of 1682 (detail, right), reliably attributed to Grinling Gibbons, features cherubs cavorting among flowers, fir cones and other natural objects.

*Within and without, the rebuilt church is dignified and elegant.
The shafts of the limestone-faced clustered piers, linked by concrete triforium
beams, and the tall arches, emphasize the loftiness of the interior (above).
The extraordinary tester hovers over the c. 1682 pulpit, brought from
St Swithin Cannon Street (destroyed 1941). The neo-Baroque spire of 1958
(right) surmounts a complex building, with fabric from the 15th, 17th
and late 19th centuries visible externally.*

*The sturdy Saxon arch of re-used Roman tiles at the west end
of the south aisle (left) is an extraordinary survival, hidden until
clearance after the 1940 bombing. Beyond are the 1950s baptistery
and the font, with its exquisite cover.*

All Hallows has the City's most important collection of medieval brasses, and there is a brass-rubbing centre. Among the brasses is a memorial to Christopher Rawson (d. 1518) and his two wives (above). The organ (left) is a replacement of 1957, by Harrison and Harrison. The case is based on an earlier instrument by Renatus Harris, destroyed in 1940.

The Tate panel (above), depicting saints and a donor, is probably from a Flemish triptych of c. 1500. It came to the church by virtue of its association with Robert Tate, whose arms are on the panel. He was Lord Mayor of London in 1488 and is buried here. The undercroft (left) is extensive, housing fragments of Saxon crosses and a memorial to William Penn, founder of Pennsylvania, who was baptized in All Hallows. The columbarium or funerary chapel of 1925-6 (right) has a medieval altar from the Crusaders' castle at Atlit, below Mount Carmel in Israel.

ALL HALLOWS LONDON WALL

◆

ALL HALLOWS stands apart among the City's surviving churches as a pure Neoclassical building. A medieval church was replaced in 1765–7, with George Dance the Younger as architect. This was his first commission, acquired at the age of 24 on his return from six years' training in Italy. Confident in his learning, Dance produced a refined design, an early and distinctly unconventional example of restrained Neoclassicism that was later to inspire his pupil Sir John Soane. The church exhibits an 'acute feeling for simple geometrical forms' (John Summerson). It is externally severe and has an elegantly simple interior with a tunnel-vaulted nave. Following serious war damage, All Hallows was meticulously restored in 1960–2 by David Nye.

One of two surviving bells (above) from the Georgian rebuilding of All Hallows, made by Lester and Pack of the Whitechapel Bell Foundry. The diagonally coffered chancel apse (right), based on the Temple of Venus in Rome, illustrates the young Dance's dependence on Antique sources. The brass chandelier was made for the church in 1766 by Lukyn Betts.

The view from under the west gallery (left) shows the architectural simplicity of the interior. The vault springs from the engaged Ionic columns without a full entablature, a radically rational conceit in the 1760s. The pulpit is approached from a vestry founded on a bastion of London's Roman wall. Other furnishings bear witness to the later adaptation of the building for use as a library and for meetings.

Squeezed between a busy road and the line of the old City wall, Dance's brown-brick church (right) looks as forbiddingly functional as an electricity sub-station, a reminder that the Neoclassical style inspired the industrial aesthetic. The stone west tower (left) moderates the plainness. The clock was made by J. H. Borley of London Wall in 1852. The small building immediately east of the church is the parish hall of 1902, by I. H. Newton of Thornton Heath.

St Andrew Holborn

Situated well outside the City's walls, the medieval church of St Andrew survived the Great Fire unscathed. Nevertheless, dilapidation and growth in the local population led to its rebuilding in 1684-6. This is one of Wren's largest churches, and it is indisputably his. The tower aside, he started anew, producing a regularly planned and imposing basilica. Externally it is double storeyed and faced in Portland stone. The interior is carefully proportioned with the nave and aisles extending to 100 ft (30 m.) and dividing into seven bays. The church was gutted by incendiary bombs in September 1941. Following a rebuilding supervised by Seely and Paget, it reopened in 1961, the interior enriched by fittings brought from elsewhere, notably from the chapel of London's Foundling Hospital, demolished *c.* 1930.

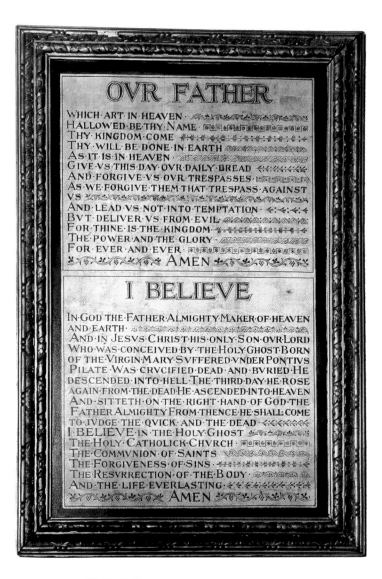

From Holborn Circus St Andrew is conspicuous (right), standing apart on the western edge of the City. Its size and the surrounding space make it unlike other City Churches. Wren retained and refaced the lower stages and buttresses of the 1459-47 west tower. The bell stage was added in 1703-4, probably by Nicholas Hawksmoor, of whom the Baroque discord in the windows is characteristic.

The 17th-century stone relief panel of the Last Judgement (above), on the north wall of the church, is said to have come from the gateway to the burial ground of the Shoe Lane workhouse. The devastation caused by the 1941 bombs is recorded in this view (left) of the east end. Seemingly lost forever, Wren's galleried basilica was resurrected in Seely & Paget's rebuilding (right). The Venetian east window has stained glass depicting the Last Supper and the Ascension, by Brian Thomas, c. 1960.

The 15th-century tower arches survive (left), re-exposed to view in a Victorian re-ordering. Beyond the north arch a Lady Chapel has been created, using part of the 1730s reredos and altar rails from St Luke Old Street; the glass is again by Thomas. The fine classical font (above) comes from the Foundling Hospital, to which it had been presented in 1804. The paschal candlestick was brought from St Mary's Abbey, West Malling in Kent.

St Andrew Undershaft

THE NAME comes from the tall shaft of the maypole that was set up nearby every year until the 16th century, when the practice was deemed pagan. This is one of the City's few complete medieval churches, dating largely from 1520-32, when rebuilding was paid for by prominent merchants, including the Merchant Taylors, Mercers and Bakers. The base of the tower and the staircase are 15th century, with the tower's distinctive pinnacles and turret added in 1883 by T. Chatfeild Clarke. Otherwise plain externally, the church is internally impressive, with a simple and regular aisled plan typical of the City's later medieval churches. It contains good decorative art and fittings in various styles. There was bomb damage in 1992, but the church is still in use for worship.

The church tower is seen (right) amid its more recent neighbours in the City, the Lloyd's and former P & O buildings. London's regenerative dynamism is not new. It was regretted by John Stow (1525-1605), London's first historian and topographer, and author of the Survey of London *(1598). His monument (above) shows him at work at his desk, with a quill pen that is regularly renewed, as if to affirm that the surveying of London is a continuing task.*

The church is rich in ornamental art by outstanding artists. A unique series of grisaille paintings of the Life of Christ (left) by Robert Brown, 1724-6, fills the spandrels of the nave arcades. At the east end (above) is Heaton, Butler and Bayne's fine Aesthetic Movement window of 1875-6, depicting the Crucifixion and the Ascension. It lights the shallow chancel (right), which has an imposing monument to Sir Thomas Offley (d. 1582), wrought-iron communion rails of 1704 by Jean Tijou and a carved reredos of 1830.

St Andrew by the Wardrobe

THE CHURCH is close to the site of the Wardrobe, where from 1361 to 1666 clothes and arms were stored by the Crown. St Andrew was one of the last of the churches lost in the Great Fire to be rebuilt, going up in 1685-94. This was a poor parish, which may account for the plainness of the church. The five-bay basilican plan is characteristic of Wren, but the economy and certain features of the design have led to a tentative attribution to Robert Hooke. Gutted by bombing in December 1940, St Andrew was rebuilt by Marshall Sisson in 1959-61. He was reasonably faithful to the earlier church, but did not attempt to replicate it. Virtually all the furnishings are replacements acquired since 1940.

The memorial to William Shakespeare (above), at one time a parishioner, was designed by Peter Foster, and carved in oak and limewood by Paul A. Cooper, c. 1990. In the 1959-61 rebuilding the aisles were panelled in to provide a chapel and offices. Thus made more domestic, the nave (right) is dominated by fine modern woodwork. The reredos, designed by Arthur Ayres, incorporates some old fabric.

Lesser-known aspects of the church include its bells (left), recast by Mears of Whitechapel in 1961, and a wooden figure of St Anne holding the Virgin and Child (above), probably north Italian, c. 1500. The public face of the church is the south elevation (right), with its commanding position above Queen Victoria Street. This route was cut through only in 1867-71, and thus the church's prominence was not originally intended; the site was formerly enclosed by housing. The tower is one of the plainest in the City.

St Anne and St Agnes

◆

Built in 1677-80, re-using the lower stages of a 14th-century tower, St Anne and St Agnes is a charming small red-brick cube of a church. It has a cross-in-square plan, representative of both Wren's documented desire to provide auditories for Protestant worship (buildings in which the whole congregation could see and hear well) and awareness of earlier 17th-century innovations in church planning in London and the Netherlands. Wren's and Hooke's respective roles here are unclear. Bomb damage in 1940 caused the loss of many fittings. A restoration by Braddock & Martin-Smith in 1963-6 involved much rebuilding and resulted in a simplified interior, reviving an essential simplicity befitting its present use for Lutheran worship.

The fine reredos (right), with its bold scrolled pediment, survived the war. It was made in c. 1680 by Mr Cheltenham, a parishioner. Many other attractive fittings have been brought in. The Lion and Unicorn fixed to the east column pedestals once stood among the pews at St Mildred Bread Street (destroyed in 1941), and the angel lectern of c. 1900 is from All Saints Bermondsey.

Inside and out, four-square symmetry is evident. The church was stuccoed in 1820, but in the 1960s the walls were largely rebuilt, reinstating red brick on two sides. These elevations are more visible than previously as a result of the creation of a small adjoining garden. The auditory interior has excellent acoustics, and the church is regularly used for concerts. The cross-in-square layout, with no chancel, satisfied 17th-century liturgical requirements as well as classical architectural sensibilities.

One of two Benefaction Boards in the church (left), publicly recording bequests to the parish, is a reminder that the City of London was once a dense aggregation of small but populous parishes.

The quality of craftsmanship in the ceiling plasterwork of this small church is evident in a detail from one corner (above).

This contrasts with the roughness of hidden spaces as seen in the tower's second stage (right), with a view through to an original doorway of a 14th-century spiral staircase.

St Bartholomew the Great

◆

St Bartholomew is a truly majestic building, the oldest in use as a London parish church. It was founded as an Augustinian priory church in 1123, with work carrying on into the 13th century. A substantial part of the 12th-century building survives, a superb and important example of Romanesque architecture. The medieval nave was pulled down after the Dissolution, and the central crossing made into the west end. Various alterations and repairs were later carried out to adapt the building for new uses: a schoolroom was created in a triforium, a smithy in a transept, and printing works in the Lady Chapel. Much of the fabric, and the external appearance of the church, is due to an extensive but careful restoration carried out by Sir Aston Webb in 1886-98.

The oriel window (above) was inserted into the choir triforium for Prior Bolton in c. 1517. It lit a private chapel, which had access from his lodgings. In a quatrefoil is Bolton's rebus, a crossbow 'bolt' piercing a wine 'tun'. A view from the crossing of the great priory church (right) shows the shadowy character of the building. Medieval painted decoration has vanished, and the Gothic furnishings are of the late 19th century.

The approach to the church is through a gateway from Smithfield, then along beside a churchyard that is the site of the original nave (above). The brick tower was added in the 1620s, and the porch, chequerwork, arcading and transepts are all Webb's. The 12th-century Romanesque choir (right) is cathedral-like in scale and coherence, and immensely sculptural in both its larger forms and its details.

The church has some Gothic features; two here are reminders of its monastic origins. The tomb chest with effigy (above) was made in c. 1405 as a memorial to Rahere (d. 1144), the prebendary of St Paul's and royal courtier, who established the priory and hospital adjoining. He was reportedly prompted to do so by a vision upon recovering from illness on his return from a pilgrimage to Rome. The priory's cloister (right) was also rebuilt in c. 1405. The eastern walk survives, restored by Webb following use as a stable.

The curve of the ambulatory at the east end of the choir (left) leads to the Lady Chapel of c. 1330. The fine screen was made by Starkie Gardner in 1897. The church has an important collection of monuments. Here (above and right) are two that reflect on war: James Rivers (d. 1641), 'Who when Ambytyon, Tyrany & Pride/Conquer'd the Age, Conquer'd Hymself & Dy'd', and the City of London Yeomanry War Memorial of c. 1920.

TO THE GLORY OF GOD AND IN PROUD AND GRATEFUL MEMORY OF THE OFFICERS NON-COMMISSIONED OFFICERS & TROOPERS OF THE CITY OF LONDON YEOMANRY (ROUGH RIDERS) WHO GAVE THEIR LIVES FOR THEIR KING AND COUNTRY IN THE GREAT WAR 1914-1918.

WE ALSO REMEMBER WITH PRIDE AND GRATITUDE THOSE WHO GAVE THEIR LIVES IN THE WAR OF 1939-1945 AND WHOSE NAMES ARE INSCRIBED ON THE SIDE PANELS.

St Bartholomew the Less

THE SMALL octagonal church is situated just inside the gates of St Bartholomew's Hospital, London's oldest hospital, established by Rahere in the reign of Henry I (1068-1135). The church provides a haven of peace and a place of worship for staff, patients and visitors to the hospital. The tower and vestry survive from a 15th-century hospital chapel, re-founded as a parish church in 1546; Inigo Jones was baptized here in 1573. The unusual octagonal nave was devised by George Dance the Younger in 1789, but it soon needed rebuilding, and was redesigned and replaced by Thomas Hardwick in 1823-5. Alterations were made in 1862-4 to designs by P. C. Hardwick, grandson of Thomas. Following war damage, Seely and Paget carried out repairs in 1950-1.

The striking star-shaped plaster rib vault (above), arising from the octagonal plan of the church, was framed in iron by Thomas Hardwick; deterioration of the 18th-century timbers necessitated early rebuilding. A view through the main hospital gate (right) looks beyond the Georgian brick and medieval stone rubble of the church to one of the ashlar ranges of James Gibbs's hospital quadrangle of 1730-59.

The view from the nave (left) into the tower, and beyond into the vestry, shows the heavily moulded 15th-century tower arches. The building houses monuments of a variety of styles and dates. The geometrical tracery in the upper windows, the pews and the alabaster pulpit were all introduced in P. C. Hardwick's 1862-4 restoration. Stained glass by Hugh Easton was installed in 1950.

IN LOVING MEMORY OF LAUNCELOT W.R. ANDREWS M.D. LOND:— DURING TWO YEARS AND A HALF A MEMBER OF THE RESIDENT STAFF OF THIS HOSPITAL WHO DIED 29 OCTOBER 1895 AGED 31 YEARS:

KEEP INNOCENCY ... UNTO THE THING THAT IS RIGHT ... SHALL BRING A MAN PEACE AT THE LAST

MAUD ANNIE MARGARET ANDREWS (SISTER JOHN) HIS WIFE DIED FEBRUARY 10ᵗᴴ 1936. AGED 74

St Benet Paul's Wharf

Sᴛ Bᴇɴᴇᴛ is a largely unaltered building of 1678–84, built in part on medieval foundations that survived the Great Fire. Formerly alongside a Thames wharf belonging to St Paul's Cathedral, the church is first recorded in 1111. Inigo Jones was buried here in 1652; a memorial designed by his protégé John Webb perished with the church in the Great Fire. The replacement building is a well-stocked box of delights, plain externally and sumptuous internally. Long attributed to Wren, it is probable that the building was in fact designed by Robert Hooke. There are drawings of both preliminary and executed designs in the latter's hand. Following proposals for its demolition, St Benet became the City's Welsh Church in 1879. Little altered at that time, it has undergone only minor works since.

The exterior (right) is domestic, small-scale and Dutch in character, with a hipped roof, red and blue chequered brickwork, carved festoons and stone quoins. The tower, with its pretty cupola based on that of St Charles Borromeo, Antwerp, is asymmetrically positioned on a re-used medieval base. Internal riches are represented by the lectern (above).

The 17th-century roof timbers (above) have remained undisturbed, and they provide valuable evidence of the building techniques and features used by Wren and his contemporaries: for example, the bolts on the wrought-iron straps. The main single-cell interior (right) has been described as 'charming in its domesticity, like a room for family prayers' (Sacheverell Sitwell). The survival of 17th-century galleries is a rarity in the City. The Royal Arms above the door are those of Charles II.

*The 17th-century furnishings are largely intact. One of the finest
pieces of furniture in any of the City Churches is the Flemish oak
communion table of c. 1660 (right), given to the church in 1686 by
Sir Leoline Jenkins, lawyer and diplomat. It has richly carved and
exquisitely draped corner caryatids, with a representation of
Charity in the centre and a bold inscription.*

Small-scale elements lend much to the overall character of the church. The shields (above) are on the front of the north gallery, which is used by the Royal College of Arms. Formerly it was used also by Doctors' Commons, a legal institution which included the Court of Admiralty (represented by the Fouled Anchor) and several ecclesiastical courts (represented by the archbishopric of Canterbury's pallium). The poor box (left) also dates from the 17th century.

St Botolph without Aldersgate

A MEDIEVAL CHURCH survived the Great Fire, its tower base and foundations partially re-used in 18th-century rebuildings: part is datable to 1754, but essentially it is of 1789-91 by Nathaniel Wright, Surveyor to the Northern District of the City of London. The east end was given a classical façade in 1829-31. Otherwise unadorned externally, the basilican church has a well-preserved late-Georgian interior of grace and distinction, with coffered apses at both ends of the main space. The Corinthian order has a continuous entablature to a vault and galleried aisles. This scheme is obviously influenced by George Dance's nearby All Hallows London Wall (page 24), idiosyncratic invention succeeding Neoclassical purity.

A view of the church in 1997 (right). The unusual decorative scheme to the east has plaster curtains and swags, a scagliola dado, and grisaille panels, all around a transparency of the Agony in the Garden, a rare survival, made by James Pearson to a design by Nathaniel Clarkson in 1788. The pews and tiled flooring are from an 1874 re-ordering by J. Blyth. The commemorative ledger stone (above) was one of several in the church floor in 1995, since covered.

The prominent east façade (above) is a Roman-cement screen with an engaged Ionic portico in channelled rustication. It was made in 1829-31, when Aldersgate Street was widened, and has been attributed to J. William Griffith, the parish surveyor. The stock-brick church is otherwise 'plain to baldness outside' (Gerald Cobb), excepting the small 18th-century bell-turret, rising in the background. A view of the repair work being undertaken in 1995 (below) illustrates the point that these buildings do not stand still.

The churchyard to the south (left) is a peaceful open space laid out as a park in the 1880s. It is known as Postman's Park from its proximity to the former General Post Office. The headstones stacked against the church (above) are a sidelined memento mori.

St Botolph Aldgate

THE CHURCH was built in 1741-4 to designs by George Dance the Elder. It replaced an early 16th-century building that itself had much earlier origins. Recent archaeology has indicated that there are burials from the 10th or 11th century under the crypt. An unassuming and sturdy Georgian brick exterior conceals an interior of special interest. Its unique character is due to the originality, vitality and elegance of the restoration effected by the eminent church architect John Francis Bentley in 1888-91. Further restoration by Rodney Tatchell followed a fire in 1965, and there have been several subsequent alterations. The church, 'more a mission to the East End than a City church' (John Betjeman), thrives as a lively centre and refuge, housing a variety of community and charitable activities.

The church contains some important 16th- and 17th-century monuments, the portrait in an aedicule (above) being one of the most colourful. It commemorates Robert Dow (d. 1612) and was made by Christopher Kingsfield in 1622-3. A view from the ritual east end (right) illustrates the squarish overall form of the interior. Bentley's essentially white restoration contrasts with darker original features such as the pulpit, communion rails and organ case.

The decorative plaster ceiling is the most remarkable feature of Bentley's inventively Gothicized Arts and Crafts scheme. The shield-carrying angels (above) are closely spaced and ornately detailed. Though out of step with the 18th-century character of the church, the ceiling does give the happy impression of being a light canopy over greater solidity below (left). Dark glass of 1857, by Charles Clutterbuck, above batik hangings of 1982, by Thetis Blacker, reverses this effect.

*T*he exterior is far more indicative of the building designed by Dance. The church is on an island site commanding one of the City's main approaches from the east. Its five-stage stock-brick tower and Portland-stone spire are prominently sited at the end of the Minories (left). The domed side-entrance lobbies derive from Wren.

St Botolph Bishopsgate

St Botolph was the patron saint of travellers, so his churches were built near City gates. Here, the medieval church survived the Great Fire, only to be rebuilt in 1725–8, for the large sum of £10,400; this was one of the City's richest parishes. Suitably 'big' designs were by James Gould, executed by a group of masons that included Gould's son-in-law, George Dance the Elder, and the latter's father, Giles Dance. Theirs is a red-brick basilican church, with an imposing stone tower and space around it. It is dignified and solidly earthbound. Later piecemeal alterations do not detract from the original character. War damage was restored by N. F. Cachemaille-Day in 1947–8. Further bomb damage in 1992–3, including the loss of stained glass, was restored in 1993–5 by Kevin Stephenson.

Detail from a war memorial (above), of mosaic and opus sectile, by William Glasby, c. 1920. The interior viewed from the chancel (right) is nobly straightforward. Giant Corinthian columns carry a sparsely decorated plaster barrel vault. The dome over the centre of the nave with lantern lighting was inserted in 1821, by Michael Meredith.

*T*o *the south is a place of retreat for office workers (above). Made into a garden in 1863, this was one of the first City churchyards so adapted. Beyond the church and in keeping with it is the parish hall, built as an infants' school in 1861. The face to Bishopsgate is of stone rather than brick (right). Exploiting the frontage, there is, unusually, an east tower, its lowest stage the chancel. The steeple in particular reflects the influence of the then recently completed Wren churches.*

Sword-rests fixed to pews are a feature of the City Churches. They were made for use by the City Swordbearer when he accompanied the Lord Mayor in state, and they carry plaques painted with mayoral coats of arms. The fine wrought-iron example (above) dates from 1855. The original panelled hexagonal pulpit (right) stands amid a clutter of later fittings.

*Above the chancel in the tower is the rope room.
It is used by the bell-ringers but otherwise seldom visited.
The three-faced clock to which the sign refers is over this
room, and its mechanism is in the old belfry the next stage
up. Above all this is the steeple.*

ST BRIDE FLEET STREET

◆

AFTER THE Great Fire the church of St Bride was rebuilt in 1671-8 to designs by Wren. It is a grand stone church, intended to be seen as above the River Fleet, and built for a parish with many wealthy residents. It was Wren's first galleried basilica, a tunnel-vaulted five-bay nave with aisles, and hugely influential. It has perhaps the most famous and elaborate of 'Wren' spires, erected in 1701-3, to designs that may in fact be by Nicholas Hawksmoor. Largely destroyed in 1940, the church was again rebuilt, by Godfrey Allen in 1955-7, with an interior departing considerably from its predecessor. The work on the 'Journalists' Church' was funded by newspapers. The excavated crypt retains important elements of Roman, Saxon and Norman work, as well as later medieval phases of construction.

The five-stage openwork Portland-stone spire (above) at 226 ft (69 m.) is the highest of all the City church spires. Said to be the original inspiration for the tiered wedding cake, it was, contrary to the adage, twice struck by lightning and rebuilt, in 1764 and again in 1803. The reredos (right) was designed by Godfrey Allen in the 1950s. An unusual feature is the stained-glass vesica. This and the trompe l'oeil painting on the east wall behind are by Glyn Jones.

Views of the pre-war interior from the west (left) and the aftermath of destruction as seen in 1941 from the east (above) are valuable records. The galleries, stained glass and box pews were not reinstated. The distinctive coupled-column arcades and the tunnel vault were renewed. An elevated view (right) shows the proximity of the church to Fleet Street, which at ground level is not obvious.

A view from the organ loft (left) shows the survival of Wren's basic form and the particularity of Allen's refitting with collegiate seating in the nave. The choir organ (right) is part of the extension organ that was built by the John Compton Company after the 1950s reconstruction. It is an important example of British organ building.

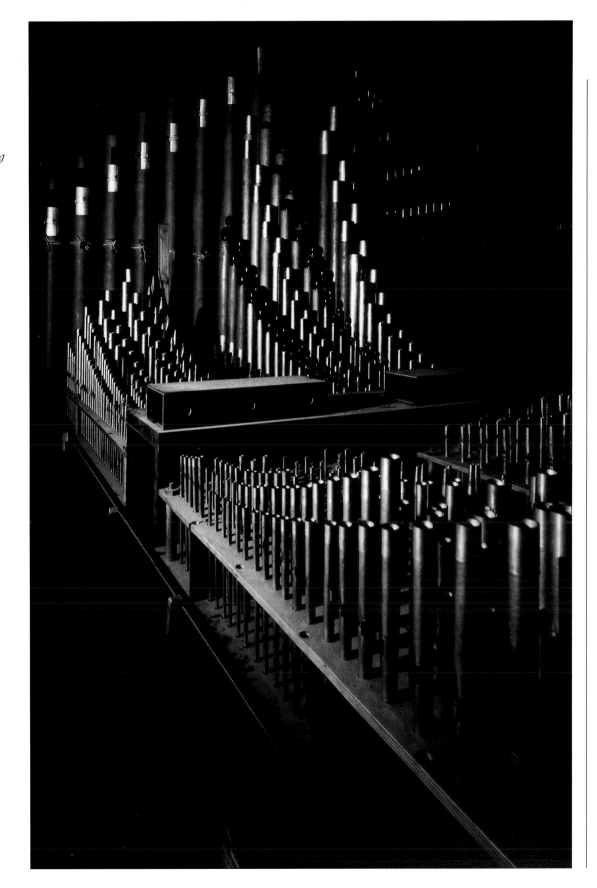

*R*emains of pre-Fire phases of building are found, and explained, in
the crypt, which extends under the raised churchyard. These remains
were revealed in 1952 in a pioneering archaeological excavation by
Professor William Grimes. The ribbed vault in the north-east corner
(above) dates from c. 1300. St Bride's bell (right) was cast by John
Taylor and Company of Loughborough. It was installed in 1955 for
full swing chiming but is no longer fitted with a bell rope.

St Clement Eastcheap

St Clement nestles amidst commercial buildings in the heart of the City's banking district. With little outward display and a single-cell interior, it is small and humble, belying its pedigree. It is a Wren rebuilding, constructed in 1683-7 to replace a church of at least 11th-century origins. The disaligned tower has medieval foundations. A modest building, 'just the sort of place that gets destroyed by administrators' (John Betjeman), the church has attracted more than its share of restorations. These have involved some of the great names of 19th- and 20th-century British church architecture — William Butterfield in 1872 and 1889, Basil Champneys in 1885-6 and 1892-3, and Sir Ninian Comper in 1932-4 — yet there is little to show for all this work. The building's chief glory remains its fine collection of original woodwork.

The late 17th-century internal fittings include much of interest. The magnificent reredos (above) was split into three by Butterfield, then reassembled, gilded and painted by Comper in the 1930s. The quoined and stuccoed tower, and west front (right), are tucked away and the building's only public face.

St Dunstan in the West

St Dunstan is an unusual pre-Revival Gothic church, octagonal and ecumenical. The medieval church narrowly survived the Great Fire. It was rebuilt when the road was widened in 1830-3 to designs by John Shaw the Elder, who died in 1832; his son, also John, finished the job. Resiting on the former churchyard helped to dictate the shape of the yellow stock-brick building. The octagon is a minor undercurrent in Georgian centralized church planning, and this is a late example. The Ketton-stone south tower is a landmark in Fleet Street, to the journalistic past of which the church has links. Inside, the church is unexpectedly spacious and remarkably little changed in its furnishings; an exception is the insertion of side-chapel altars dedicated to several Eastern Christian churches.

The 16th-century Flemish figure panels (above) have been incorporated into the surround of the main altar. A limewood iconostasis (right) marks the Orthodox Chapel of the Romanians. Brought from Antim Monastery, Bucharest, in 1966, it was carved by Petre and Mihai Babic in 1860-3, with paintings by Petre Alexandrescu.

The altar in the Orthodox Chapel of the Romanians (left), behind the iconostasis, is under an 1895 stained-glass window by C. E. Kempe & Company. The lightness of the star-ribbed vault (above) is in part due to concealed structural iron. The church has a good collection of monuments. The brass with kneeling figures (right) commemorates Henry Dacres, 'Merchant Taylor and sumtyme Alderman of London', and his wife (d. 1530).

The scale of the interior is evident in this view across the nave (left). Over the main altar to the north the ritual east window retains only tracery lights from Thomas Willement's stained glass of 1852, the rest having been destroyed in 1944. The pulpit and the box pews survive from 1830-3. The intricate and beautiful lantern on the tall south tower (above) is based on that at All Saints Pavement, York. The clock, made in 1671 by Thomas Harris, was moved in 1828, then brought back by Viscount Rothermere in 1935. Its Ionic aedicule houses two bell-strikers, said to represent Gog and Magog.

Statues of King Lud and his sons in the vestry porch (left) are from Lud Gate, once the main western entrance into the City of London, said to have been built by King Lud in 66 BC but more plausibly erected in 1586. The gate was demolished in 1760. From spaces behind the scenes are views of the organ (above) and the crypt (right). Splendid 1830s brickwork leads to a vault with compartments for coffins, long-since cleared.

St Edmund King and Martyr

◆

St Edmund, King of East Anglia, was killed by the Danes in 870. His medieval church was lost in the Great Fire and was entirely replaced in 1670-4 to designs reliably assigned to Robert Hooke. It is a handsome church, but not big, with something of a formal stone frontispiece to Lombard Street that has Continental echoes in the parapets rising up beside the tower. Behind there is a single-cell open-plan interior. The 1670s construction was not entirely successful, defects leading to alterations to the tower and the building of a new steeple in 1706-7, designed by Hawksmoor. The church has twice suffered bomb damage, in 1917 and 1941; repairs were carried out in 1929-32 by Caröe and Passmore, and in 1957 and 1968 by Rodney Tatchell.

To the north, the ritual east window depicting Christ in Glory (above) came to the church by a complicated route. It was reportedly manufactured in Munich in the 1860s and intended for St Paul's. Rejected by the cathedral, the glass went instead to St Bartholomew Moor Lane, and when that church was demolished, c. 1905, it was brought to St Edmund. A view in the bell chamber (right) shows a precarious way up to the timber-framed steeple.

*U*nder a remade ceiling, there
is much fine woodwork (above).
There are two organ cases, one
of 1701-2 and the other, built in
1880, a replica. An elliptical
rail with twisted balusters
surrounds the marble font
(right), which is decorated with
carvings of acanthus leaves.
Both rail and font are original.

*T*hough now reattributed to
Hooke and to Hawksmoor, the
church was, as with all the
post-Fire churches, built under
Wren's supervision. Its presence
in the street (right) has gained
in gravity from the 1929-32
refacing in ashlar of the
formerly brick east return wall.

St Ethelburga Bishopsgate

◆

St Ethelburga, first abbess of Barking, was the daughter of Ethelbert, in the 7th century the first Christian King of Kent. Her only church was laid waste in April 1993 by a terrorist bomb, a sad loss to London. The tiny church, only 55 ft (17 m.) long and 30 ft (9 m.) high, was a unique survivor of the once-numerous small medieval City Churches, most of which were lost in the Great Fire. The building of *c.* 1390 appears to have replaced one with 12th-century origins, to judge from carved stones found in excavations made in 1994. Its diminutive ragstone rubble front, incongruously squeezed between gigantic office blocks, was blown away by the blast. However, the four-bay south arcade remains standing, as do the south and east walls. The form of their rehabilitation in a new building has been the subject of much debate.

These views are effectively a pictorial epitaph. The jumble of scaffolding (above) shows the site of the church in 1995. A view of the east end c. 1920 (right) portrays the lost interior. The intricate Gothic rood screen of 1912 was designed by Sir Ninian Comper. The parclose screen beyond was salvaged in 1995.

St Giles Cripplegate

At the heart of the modern precinct that is the Barbican Estate is St Giles, a very late Perpendicular church built in *c.* 1550 and thus representing the last gasp of the medieval tradition. Externally it appears fairly homogeneous, but its building history is complex. An earlier medieval church appears to have been rebuilt in *c.* 1390, then all but wholly rebuilt again following a fire in 1545, perhaps re-using the earlier plan. At both ends survive walls of the 14th century. The tower was raised in brick in 1682-4. Between 1884 and 1905 the church was heavily restored and refaced in ragstone. After severe bomb damage in 1940, it was again restored, by Godfrey Allen, and reopened in 1960.

The church has been refurnished since the war with a curious mixture of objects, many made recently, in traditional form. The sword-rest (right) attests to continuity in City ceremonial. The sculpted bust (above) depicts John Bunyan, author of Pilgrim's Progress, *who worshipped here. It is one of a set from the Cripplegate Institute, presented by J. Passmore Edwards, c. 1900. The others represent John Milton (buried here), Oliver Cromwell (married here) and Daniel Defoe (died nearby).*

THE · RT · HON

SIR · PETER · STUDD · LORD · MAYOR

1970

LORD · MAYOR

THE

RT · HON

The setting of the church has been dramatically transformed. A pre-war view (above) shows early timber houses. Wiped out by bombing, the Barbican area was comprehensively redeveloped from 1956 onwards to powerful Modernist designs by Chamberlin, Powell & Bon (right). With the 400 ft (120 m.) apartment towers behind, and the piazza, lake, gas lamps and fragments of old City wall in the foreground, the church is now strangely placed, like a ship in dry dock.

At the west end of the north aisle (right) is a fine font with acanthus decoration and a wooden cover, brought here from St Luke Old Street (roof removed 1959). The window behind, commemorating the 1991 centenary of the Cripplegate Foundation, depicts the old City gate with recent high-rise buildings beyond. In the tower (left) is a fine set of twelve bells made by Mears and Stainbank in 1953.

The heavily restored interior (right) is austere, dominated by finely moulded nave arcading. The chancel arch was remade in 1858-9 after Georgian alterations. The east window is by Allen, based on evidence for its 14th-century form, with glass by A. K. Nicholson Studios, inserted in 1957. The arch-braced roof is also post-war.

St Helen Bishopsgate

S<small>T</small> H<small>ELEN HAS</small> a long history of
alterations, the building having been
adapted to uses running from the
conventual to the evangelical. It is one
of the City's few medieval churches,
with unusual origins as two distinct
builds. A Benedictine nunnery was
founded in *c.* 1210, and the nuns'
choir was built parallel to an existing
parish church. It became a place
where 'the daughters of the merchant
princes took the veil'(*Survey of
London*). Rebuilding in several phases
culminated in *c.* 1475 in a rectangular
double nave with a south transept.
Subsequent phases of alteration
complicated appearances. Then serious
bomb damage in 1992 and 1993 led to
further change. In 1995 a controversial
re-ordering to designs by Quinlan
Terry provided double the seating.
This is a church where preachers
often attract a large congregation.

*The church is rich in fittings and monuments from before the Great
Fire, including the earliest surviving sword-rest in the City. This is
made of wood and is dated 1665. At its head (above) angels flank the
arms of Sir John Lawrence, Lord Mayor in 1665. The bells (right)
stand in a little timber turret at the west end of the church. Their
frame, first constructed in 1568-9, was remade in 1696.*

The 1995 re-ordering was radical in its effect on the interior. An earlier photograph (above) shows the raised chancel at the east end of the south range or parish church. The Perpendicular Gothic screen and the reredos were introduced by J. L. Pearson in 1891-3 in an elegant High Anglican restoration. Pearson also repositioned the pulpit, another rare example of pre-Fire woodwork, dating perhaps from a c. 1632-3 phase of alterations in a crude classical style known as 'Artisan Mannerist'.

Viewed from a new west gallery, the 1995 interior (above) is spacious and filled with light, without the nooks and crannies of its earlier layout (opposite). The east windows replace stained-glass windows lost in 1992. The arcade dividing the once-separate sections is of c. 1475, with earlier arches to the east.

The pulpit remains as positioned by Pearson, but his screen has been turned to form a partition to the monument-encrusted south transept. A doorcase in the transept (right) has been moved from the south wall of the nave.

*A*lterations notwithstanding, this remains a medieval church, distinguished by its outstanding collection of early monuments. Late 14th-century alabaster effigies of John de Oteswich and his wife (right), moved from St Martin Outwich (demolished 1874), and brasses of Thomas Wylliams (d. 1495) and his wife (above), emphasize the flowing robes of medieval costume. Hidden off Bishopsgate, the slightly asymmetrical west end (left) corresponds to the twin interiors. There is a 14th-century doorway to the south, or right, windows of c. 1475, and a 16th-century doorway to the north, or left.

St James Garlickhythe

GARLICKHYTHE WAS the wharf in the medieval port where garlic was landed, but embanking has long since taken the river away from the church. The medieval St James was replaced in 1676-84 to designs almost certainly by Wren. The church is neatly planned, a simple rectangle with implied transepts in the middle bay to suggest a cross, a free adaptation of the form of some pre-Restoration London churches. The combination of the traditional east-west liturgical axis with centralization for an auditory was an elegant reconciliation of medieval tradition with the liturgical demands and classicism of the 17th century, a challenge for architects across Europe. St James has a tidy domesticity to its internal arrangements. It has been well refurnished and was skilfully restored in the 1950s by David Lockhart Smith and Alexander Gale.

The tall and brightly lit nave (right) has a Father Smith organ of 1687. This has a splendid case with trumpeting cherubs and the scallop shell of St James. The pulpit with its tester was introduced in 1878, having come from the demolished St Michael Queenhithe, as did the stalls with their carved backs. The clock (above) is from the tower's west front, a 1988 replica of one destroyed in the Blitz.

The photograph from 1991 (left) shows the aftermath of an accident in which a crane fell through the centre bay of the church. The damage has been wholly repaired. The ornate Baroque steeple (above) was built in 1714-17 at the end of the City Church rebuilding programme, 50 years after the Great Fire. Its graceful design has been attributed to Hawksmoor.

The church has the heavy traffic of Upper Thames Street to its south, but relative tranquillity in the form of an arboreal open space at the foot of Garlick Hill immediately to the west; from this point (right) there is a view of the west doorcase in the tower. The iron railings and openwork grapevine piers were given by the Vintners' Company in c. 1965.

ST KATHERINE CREE

◆

CHURCHES FROM the reign of Charles I (1625-49) are rare, and St Katherine, rebuilt in 1628-31 save for its tower, is, for this reason, especially fascinating. Erected under the patronage of Bishop William Laud, it is tempting to see the church as a manifestation of the Laudian return to pre-Reformation liturgical practice, which required a longitudinal axis. However, its longitudinal form may simply have been a perpetuation of the site's typical late-medieval plan. What is truly striking is the free mixture of Gothic and classical architectural elements. The styles are arrestingly juxtaposed in a manner that may be more typical of the time than conventional stylistic classifications would allow. This exceptional church escaped the Great Fire and has undergone only minor works since.

A view from the organ gallery (right) shows the axial nature of the layout, so unlike Wren's auditory churches of 50 years later. The Corinthian arcades march along to the Gothic east window, distinct but coherent. The rose (here usually called a Catherine wheel) has rare stained glass of 1630; the lower lights are of 1876. The Gothic ribbed plaster ceilings have bosses bearing the arms of City Livery Companies.

*T*he church faces on to Leadenhall Street (above). The unusual
flat-headed tripartite windows have classical aprons and taller centre lights,
a motif used elsewhere in the early to mid 17th century that resembles a
Gothicized Venetian window. The south-west tower survives from c. 1504,
with some fragmentary 15th-century fabric. The west window was blocked
in for the insertion of the organ in 1686. The upper stage of the tower
and the cupola were rebuilt in 1776.

Cherubs decorate the finely carved Father Smith organ case of 1686 (left). Purcell and Handel are both said to have played the organ here.

The octagonal marble font (above), with its knobbly ornament and ogee-domed cover, is probably from c. 1631. It bears the arms of Sir John Gayer, an East India merchant and Lord Mayor, who endowed St Katherine's annual 'Lion Sermon' as a thanksgiving for his survival after an encounter with a lion.

St Lawrence Jewry

In a part of the City occupied by Jews until their expulsion from England in 1290 is what has become the Guild Church of the Corporation of London. It stands with space around it at one corner of Guildhall Yard, the ancient centre of London's local government. Expensively rebuilt in 1671-80 by Wren and Hooke, St Lawrence has stone elevations and a wide single-cell interior with a north aisle. The church was gutted in 1940. Cecil Brown undertook the rebuilding in 1954-7, adopting a painstaking and lavish late 17th-century manner. An aura of polish accords with mayoral dignity and use of the church for Guildhall ceremonial; 'very municipal, very splendid' (John Betjeman).

A window of 1959-60 by Christopher and John Webb (above) depicts Sir Christopher Wren, flanked by Grinling Gibbons, woodcarver, and Edward Strong, stonemason, representing the craftsmen who worked on the City Churches under Wren. The north aisle (right) has become the Commonwealth Chapel, as the flags illustrate. The two-part organ was built by Noel Mander in 1957.

Viewed from the north east (right), the church presents Guildhall Yard with its plainest front, the only one built in rubble. A lane once passed by, and intervening buildings have been cleared. Beyond is a recent extension to the Guildhall. The somewhat dumpy tower has obelisk pinnacles and a spire that is a faithful replacement of its 1670s predecessor. The Lord Mayor has his own pew, with a sword-rest (above), in front of those for City Aldermen.

The north gallery, removed in 1866-7, was not reinstated by Brown in the 1950s. Instead he provided an elaborate screen to create a north chapel (above). He designed most of the fittings himself, and the craftsmanship is of a high quality. Dark oak stands out against white, grey and gold, the effect enhanced by the bold silhouettes of the extraordinary angels. The ironwork screens of 1974 and later were made in the workshops of the Royal Electrical and Military Engineers.

St Magnus the Martyr

◆

Hard by London Bridge, St Magnus was one of the first churches to burn in 1666. It was rebuilt in 1668-84, initially by the parish, with Wren becoming involved only from 1671. The steeple was added in 1703-6. A complex series of alterations has obscured the original form more than in any other Wren church, disguising what was probably subtle centralized planning. After a fire in 1760 the upper parts were rebuilt by Peter Biggs. Within a decade further substantial alterations were made by George Dance the Younger. The interior, which had become an aisled basilica, was richly transformed for Anglo-Catholic worship in 1924-5 in a Continental Baroque restoration by Martin Travers.

The worn stone flags of the entrance lobby evoke long and heavy use (right). The statue of St Magnus (above), holding the church, was made by Martin Travers in 1925. Magnus is the name of 11 Christian martyrs, and it is not clear to which one the church is dedicated.

*B*uilt to be a landmark at the end of London Bridge, the grand 185 ft (56 m.) tower (above) is powerfully monumental. The design derives from St Charles Borromeo in Antwerp. What John Betjeman called 'the insolent neo-Egyptian bulk of Adelaide House' creates a tension with the tower that is exciting rather than deflating. Following a series of alterations, little of the interior (right) can safely be ascribed to Wren. The sparing linear plasterwork of the vault is probably late Georgian.

The pulpit (above), with its great glowering tester, and the comparably splendid reredos were reconstructed by Travers. Music-stands grace the west gallery (left and right), the projecting centre of which complements the vault. Several phases in the building's complex history are represented here. The gallery was perhaps created at the same time as the organ was installed, in 1712; inscriptions above the octagonally glazed screen of c. 1760 commemorate repairs in 1886 and 1924-5.

ST MARGARET LOTHBURY

◆

St MARGARET STANDS opposite the Bank of England. Behind the sober exterior lies a treasure house, with numerous fittings displaying exquisite craftsmanship, many of them brought from demolished City Churches. The foundations of a medieval church that had been rebuilt in 1440 were re-used by Wren in a further rebuilding of 1683-92. The tower and steeple were not completed until 1698-1700. The interior is an irregular rectangle, with a south aisle. Substantial re-ordering in the 1890s by Walter Tapper of the firm Bodley and Garner introduced fittings from St Olave Jewry (demolished 1888) and All Hallows the Great (demolished 1894), among them a particularly elaborate chancel screen from All Hallows.

The portrait bust (above) of Alderman John Boydell (d.1804), engraver and print publisher, and Lord Mayor, was designed by Thomas Banks in 1791, and carved by F. W. Smith in 1820, for St Olave Jewry. The chapel in the south aisle (right) was formed by Tapper in the 1890s following removal of a gallery. The late 17th-century font, also from St Olave Jewry, has a relief of Noah's Ark.

The Portland-stone south front of the church faces squarely on to Lothbury (right), in a line of buildings that includes the handsome bankers' classicism of the 1932 Royal Bank of Canada, Venetian Gothic from 1866, and the 1960s Modernist Stock Exchange beyond. The clean-cut south-west tower in four stages has a pleasing slender obelisk steeple that has been attributed to Hooke.

The All Hallows screen (above) is one of only two 'Wren' screens in the City. Made in 1683-4, with virtuoso carving and piercing, it has openwork pilasters and balusters, and Royal Arms in an open pediment with an eagle below. Another view of the superbly carved font (right), traditionally attributed to Grinling Gibbons, shows other religious scenes: St Philip baptizing the eunuch, and Adam and Eve in the Garden of Eden.

The pulpit (above) is one of the few indigenous features. Yet its striking tester, with fine openwork carving, comes from All Hallows the Great. The reredos and communion table in the south aisle (right) come from St Olave Jewry; the Annunciation was painted in 1908 by Sister Catherine Weeks. The wood and wrought-iron parclose screen of 1891 was designed by W. Rowlands Ingram, brother of the rector at the time; it incorporates communion rails from St Olave Jewry.

St Margaret Pattens

This is a modest building, though it proclaims itself with an eyecatching spire. The name may be connected with the making of wooden shoes in the Middle Ages in a nearby lane. The medieval church was rebuilt in 1538, then again by Wren in 1684-7 re-using earlier foundations. He provided a single-cell rectangular interior with a north aisle. The spire was added in 1698-1702. There have been no major alterations, though the interior was re-ordered in 1879-80. Another minor restoration was undertaken in 1955-6, when the building was made a Guild Church. It accommodates offices for a charity, and is used from time to time for musical performances.

Outside stands a brightly painted cast-iron bollard (above). Inside, a view to the west (right) is dominated by the organ of 1749. Over the entrance are the finely carved Royal Arms of James II. On either side are churchwardens' pews, uniquely canopied, one dated 1686. Two were required once the neighbouring parish of St Gabriel Fenchurch had to be accommodated after 1666.

An early view of the church in its commercial setting (right) emphasizes its prickly verticality. The tall, 199 ft (60 m.) leaded timber spire and stone angle pinnacles to the tower are, for the date, unexpectedly medieval in style. By contrast, the south front has an appealing and typically Wren medley of round and rounded architraves. The lectern eagle (above) has the unusual detail of a viper grasped in its talons.

The Della Robbia tondo (left) is incorporated into the reredos of the north-aisle chapel. This reredos was installed by James Fish, a neo-Jacobite rector in the late 19th-century, to commemorate Thomas Wagstaffe, rector from 1684 to 1689, who was deprived of the living because of his loyalty to James II. A detail that is more indicative of low-church practice is the iron hourglass stand on the pulpit (above), a reminder of the length of sermons. The geometry of the interior was simplified in 1955-6, when the north gallery was enclosed.

ST MARTIN LUDGATE

St MARTIN was rebuilt in 1677–86, incorporating part of the Roman City wall in its west side. The architect is likely to have been Hooke, documented as having paid 31 visits to the site. Hooke is said to have been influenced by Netherlandish architecture, and the church has echoes of buildings on the Continent. The south front on Ludgate Hill, an important feature in the western approach to St Paul's Cathedral, is symmetrically composed as a frontispiece rising up to a 'Dutch' spire. Inside, a narthex, or vestibule, separates the street from the auditorium. The latter has a cross-in-square plan, to a space that is proportionally rather tall. With fine dark woodwork, this is among the City's least altered 17th-century interiors. It survived the war and has been only lightly restored.

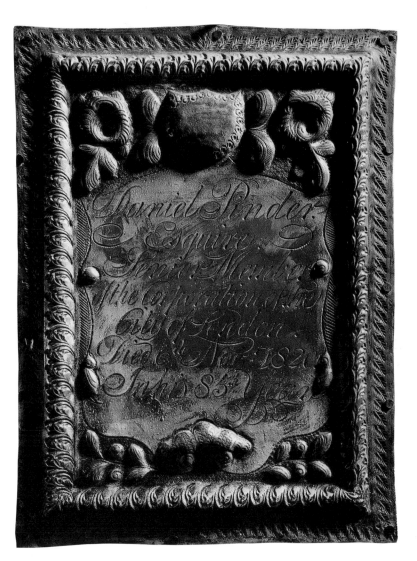

The structural complexity of the framed spires of the City Churches is seen by few. A dense web of timber frames the lower stage in St Martin's spire (right). The spiral staircase leads to a balcony surrounding the open stage that supports the needle spirelet. The embossed lead coffin plate (above) is displayed inside the church.

The centralized auditory interior (left) retains the original box pews, cut down in height and converted to benches by Ewan Christian in 1894-5. This has left the plinths to the four Composite columns looking strangely tall. The reredos is also original, as are the hexagonal pulpit (with later stairs) and the screen across the coffered south arcade with its three superb doorcases. The scrolls of the Portland-stone façade on Ludgate Hill (above) draw the eye upwards.

*T*he font (right) is another
early feature; indeed, it predates
the church, having been made
in 1673, presumably for the
temporary 'tabernacle' that was
used before and during
rebuilding. Its fleshy forms are
somehow at odds with its Greek
inscription, translatable as
'cleanse my sins and not only
my face'. To one side of the font
is a marble Pelican in her
Piety, a symbol of Christ's
sacrifice. The bell (above) dates
from 1693 and stands on an
iron chest. The late 19th-
century glass (left) was made
by James Powell & Sons
of Whitefriars.

St Mary Abchurch

REBUILT TO designs by Wren in 1681–6, St Mary Abchurch is widely acknowledged to be the least altered of the churches built after the Fire. It is an architectural glory, 'both uplifting and intimate' (John Betjeman), its interior based on the simple geometry of a circle on a square. A seemingly weightless saucer dome creates dramatic grandeur within a small compass. Of the surviving Wren churches, only St Stephen Walbrook (page 212) creates a comparable effect. Furthermore, the church is rich in original carved and pierced woodwork. Following war damage, which led to the discovery of a previously concealed medieval vaulted chamber under the churchyard, the church was sensitively repaired by Godfrey Allen in 1946–58.

Near the entrance to the church is an alms box made in 1694 (above). The nave (right) is wholly and simply covered by the painted dome, unique in a City church. Foremost among the fittings is the splendid reredos, the only one in the City actually documented as having been carved by Grinling Gibbons, who was paid for the 'olter pees' in 1686.

*T*he dome overhead represents the immortal, the vaults beneath the mortal; between them lies the urban. The Heavenly Choir around the Name of God in Hebrew (left) was painted by a parishioner, William Snow, in 1708-9, for the sum of £170. A stern message (below) is mounted over the entrance to the rediscovered medieval vault. Before the the red-brick south front (right) is an area of patterned paving, laid down in 1877 in what was once the churchyard, to form a felicitous open space.

The 1680s timber framing of the cupola (left), on which stands the lantern and spire, has specially selected sinuous braces for the ogee. The marble font (above) is another survival from 1686, the architectural cover being a pavilion with statuettes of the four Evangelists. The view to the south door (right), with its richly carved aedicular doorcase, shows the pierced-fronted churchwardens' pews.

ST MARY ALDERMARY

◆

THIS APPEARS to be a marvel, a 'Tudor' church of 1679-82. It is the only church rebuilt under Wren that is in the Gothic style. It probably had Saxon origins and had been rebuilt in *c.* 1510, the tower only completed in 1629. The ground plan of that building, with sections of masonry including the lower stages of the tower, survived the Great Fire. Wren's task was thus more reconstruction than replacement. The tower had to be rebuilt in 1701-4, work that was undertaken by William Dickinson, who was then engaged in repairs to Westminster Abbey and who had a predilection for the Gothic. In 1876 the church was externally refaced and embellished, and internally thoroughly re-ordered, by Richard Tress and Charles Innes.

The plaster fan vaulting of 1679-82 over the nave (above) might have been loosely based on what existed there before, though it has more in common with 18th-century Gothick plasterwork than with anything of the 16th century. The origin of the design for the dramatic tower (right) is also debatable. However interpreted, these features illustrate the endurance of the Gothic style through the 17th and into the 18th century.

*The church has a large six-bay double-aisled interior (left).
Its Gothic arcades are formed of slender four-shaft piers
carrying 'Tudor' arches, with classical plasterwork in the
spandrels. One of few remaining early fittings is the classical
font of 1682 (above); another is the west doorcase, from
St Antholin Watling Street (demolished 1876). The dogmatically
Gothic Revival 1876 re-ordering replaced many other classical
fittings in a manner inconsistent with the spirit of
the late 17th-century building.*

*The vestry (above) has 18th-century oak panelling with enriched
panels over the fireplace and on the north wall. The table and chairs
are also of oak, in a 17th-century style. There is an octagonal
rooflight and, out of view, the room has four safes inscribed with the
names of the four parishes that formerly used the church.*

An early photograph (left) shows the church at the time of the building of Queen Victoria Street around 1870. This reveals the virtual separation of the tower from the nave and aisles; the whole has been summed up as 'straightforward late Perpendicular' (B. F. L. Clarke), an apt oxymoron. Beyond is a glimpse of St Paul's. The wooden sword-rest (above) is dated 1682.

St Mary le Bow

St Mary stands at the heart of the City, on Cheapside, the main shopping street of medieval London. There may have been a vaulted stone church here from as early as *c.* 1090; a substantial crypt survives. The church housed the Archbishop of Canterbury's Court of Arches, and from *arcubus* comes Bow. After the Fire, St Mary was one of the first City Churches attended to by Wren, being built in 1668-80. It is one of his acclaimed masterpieces and, at £15,645, was the costliest of the new churches. Wren introduced an innovative Neoclassical plan and resited the tower to be prominent on Cheapside. The church was burned out in 1941, though the crypt and steeple survived. Rebuilding in 1954-64 was to designs by Lawrence King.

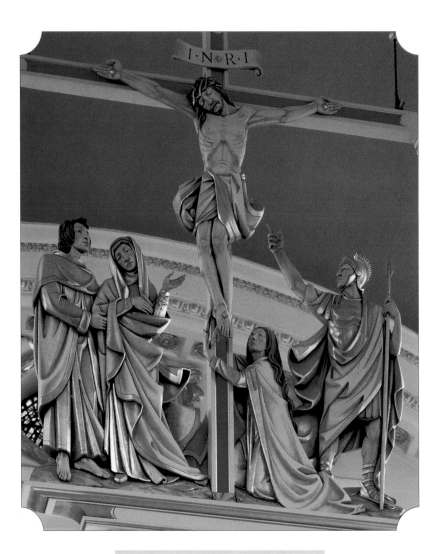

The Baroque tower and steeple of Portland stone (right) contrast markedly with the simple brick exterior of the nave. This was the first classical steeple in London and at 224 ft (68 m.) a prominent landmark — the exemplar against which later steeples were to be judged. The suspended rood of the Crucifixion (above) was carved in Oberammergau and given by the people of Germany.

*T*he double-aisled auditory
interior (right), squarish and
without a chancel, was based by
Wren on the Basilica of
Maxentius in Rome, which he
knew only from books. After
war damage, seen in a view of
the west wall looking towards
St Paul's (above), it was
entirely rebuilt. Traditionally,
the true cockney was born
within the sound of Bow bells,
seen from above (left).

The stained-glass windows at the east end (above) were made by John Hayward in 1963-4 as part of King's Modernist overhaul. They replace windows seen in a pre-1941 view of the elliptically vaulted interior (left), which had been much re-ordered in 1867.

The large Norman crypt comprising a nave and two aisles bears witness to the size and status of the early building. Perhaps constructed by a Canterbury workshop, the nave of three bays by four has columns with cushion capitals (below). Closed up, it was rediscovered and revaulted by Wren. Again reconstructed around 1960, the crypt comprises the Chapel of the Holy Spirit (left), the Court of Arches, and the Common Room. With a busy restaurant, this is architecturally and atmospherically a very different place from the church above.

The rebuilt interior, viewed from the organ gallery (left), owes its overall shape to Wren, but its details date from c. 1960. The free-standing altar reflects modern liturgy, and the arcade keystones depict the heads of the bishop, architect and others involved in the rebuilding. The reredos and panelling were made by Faithcraft. A classic view along Cheapside (above) shows the tower and the sublime proportions of its steeple.

ST MARY AT HILL

A DISTINCTLY interesting Wren church, St Mary is one of the least fortunate survivors, having suffered many fires. Rebuilding in 1670-4 re-used much medieval fabric, with the north and south walls of *c.* 1490–1500 simply raised and refenestrated. The domed cross-in-square plan is the earliest instance of auditory central planning after the Fire. This form may have been based around transepts in the earlier building. If so, this only strengthens a sense of Wren's adaptable inventiveness. However, the church was much remade in the 19th century, and its precise 1670s form is uncertain. A serious fire in 1988 necessitated another restoration, carried out in 1990-2 by the Conservation Practice (architect John Barnes). Refitting after these repairs had not been carried out at the time of photography in 1995.

The cherub (above) is from the upper part of the ex situ reredos, the dating of the disparate pieces of which is difficult. There was some refitting in the early 18th century and in 1848-9, when William Gibbs Rogers restored fire damage with furnishings very convincingly in the style of Wren. A view downhill to Billingsgate Market (right) shows the stuccoed east end of the church, its only prominent elevation.

A photograph of the aftermath of the 1988 fire (above) shows the ruinous interior, much of which had been remade by James Savage in 1826-7. He introduced round-headed windows and the vaults, and heightened the dome. The plasterwork is his, but the Composite columns, based on a pattern by Serlio, are of the 1670s. Uniquely for a church in the City, the box pews were still in place in the 1980s, as was the reredos and an 1848-9 pulpit.

The rebuilt interior looking east (left) has the dome and vaults remade, but the pews, reredos and pulpit not yet reinstated. The removal of this woodwork left what had been 'the least spoiled and the most gorgeous interior in the City' (John Betjeman) with an antiseptic and unintentionally Postmodern feel. The c. 1600 relief panel of the Resurrection (far left, bottom) is mounted in the porch, having once been over the churchyard entrance.

St Mary Woolnoth

This, the only complete City church by Hawksmoor, is a powerfully effective and highly original building. Its predecessors may have been founded in the 11th century, by Wulfnoth; hence the name. The church was poorly rebuilt around its medieval remains in 1670–5. A clause added to the 1711 'Fifty New Churches' Act underwrote rebuilding from scratch in 1716–27. Hawksmoor's prominent stone exterior is outstandingly inventive. The interior is centralized, a square within a square. This volumetric composure combines with a characteristic compression of forms to produce Baroque tension; unusually, this is rectilinear rather than diagonal or sinuous. The church was self-effacingly restored by William Butterfield in 1875–6.

The magnificently muscular north elevation (right) loses nothing when compared with the best of Continental Baroque architecture. Facing Lombard Street, it is essentially urban as it depends on proximity for its effect. To keep street noise out of the church there are no windows, so dramatic effect is the elevation's sole justification. The nave ceiling (above), seen with a clerestory window, is more static in its forms.

Great Corinthian columns in clusters of three mark out the square nave (left). The reredos, in the form of a baldacchino in the manner of Bernini, and the bulbous pulpit, its tester reflecting the shape of the ceiling, are original fittings. The unorthodox gallery fronts and piers, evidently valued by Butterfield, were retained and set back against the side walls when he removed the galleries. The Royal Arms and the reredos lettering are from 1968. A passage leading to the tower (above) forms a humble but intricate space.

This view of the church from the south (left) was not possible until King William Street was built in 1829-35. The plainer five-bay side originally faced an alley. The screen in front was built for Bank Underground Station in 1897-1900. Hawksmoor's idiosyncratic twin-turreted tower and the clerestory 'box' over the nave, are further manifestations of his rectilinear Baroque. Within the tower the bells (above) are housed in separate timber frames. The cherub keystone (right) is jammed between triglyphs, another piece of Baroque playfulness.

ST MICHAEL CORNHILL

◆

THIS CHURCH is like a palimpsest, its architects having devised successive combinations of the classical and the Gothic. A Saxon foundation, St Michael was an important medieval church. It was rebuilt in 1669-72 by the parish around surviving fabric that included a large 1420s tower. Working too early to have involved Wren, 'skilful workmen' replaced the Gothic nave and aisles in classical form. In 1857-60 Sir George Gilbert Scott transformed St Michael with the first thorough High Victorian restoration in the City. For a time reviled, it is now considered to be among the best Victorian work in the City Churches. An 'early Basilican style' was ingeniously adopted as the best method of making a classical interior more 'Christian' without resort to pointed forms. Outside all is Gothic.

The simple four-bay interior of 1669-72 (right) has Tuscan arcades and groin vaults. It was comprehensively refitted by Scott in 1857-60; the pulpit and pews were made by William Gibbs Rogers, and the timber angel corbels by John Birnie Philip. Christ in Glory (above), from the east window, is part of an excellent 1858 scheme of stained glass by John Clayton and Alfred Bell, probably carried out by Heaton & Butler.

The massive Portland-stone tower was rebuilt in 1715-22 (left). William Dickinson designed the tower's lower stages, the corner turrets suggesting respect for, if not part retention of, 1420s work. The more elaborate upper parts were added by Hawksmoor. Scott's Italianate reredos (right), Cosmati work of alabaster with marble inlay, incorporates 17th-century paintings of Aaron and Moses by Robert Streeter. The wrought-iron communion rails are of 1857-60. The Pelican in her Piety (above) was carved in 1775 for the 17th-century reredos.

*The pews, with poppy-head bench ends in a medieval manner (above),
are good examples of Rogers's skilful 1850s carving. Scott gave
St Michael an ornate 'Franco-Italian Gothic' north porch to face
Cornhill (right); otherwise the exterior at street level is all but concealed.
The tympanum, richly carved by Philip, shows 'St Michael Disputing
with Satan about the Body of Moses'. The bronze War Memorial of 1920
is by Richard Goulden, depicting St Michael driving away War.*

St Michael Paternoster Royal

St Michael's full name derives from the former proximity of paternoster (rosary) makers, and La Réole, a house called after a Gascon wine town. Sir Richard Whittington, merchant, philanthropist, four times Lord Mayor and, most famously since, Christmas pantomime hero, had a house next door. In 1409 he paid for the church to be rebuilt. Wren's rebuilding of 1685-94 was one of his last City Churches. Its simple exterior has a delightful steeple, added in 1713-17, one of several steeples re-attributed to Hawksmoor. Following bomb damage in 1944, the single-cell rectangular interior was altered in the last post-war City Church restoration, carried out in 1964-8 by Elidir Davies for the Missions to Seamen.

The Dick Whittington window (right) is part of a big, bright 1968 stained-glass scheme by John Hayward. Whittington has his emblematic and mythical cat, and is 'so garbed as to suggest Sherlock Holmes or a gamekeeper' (Gerald Cobb). The Royal Arms of William III are an original feature. The fine and unusual statue of Aaron (above) came from the reredos of All Hallows the Great, demolished in 1894.

*T*he proportions of the interior (left) were altered in 1964-8 when offices were inserted behind the organ; the case is a replica of one of 1749, with a new instrument made by Noel Mander. The statue of Charity trampling Avarice (above) was made in 1992, to replace a stolen piece. The view along College Street (right) indicates the tranquil setting and shows the building's glory, its particularly delicate steeple, the lower stage of which is encircled by eight projecting Ionic columns.

St Nicholas Cole Abbey

St NICHOLAS has become Cole Abbey Presbyterian Church, in use since 1982 by the Free Church of Scotland. There is nothing abbatial in its history. The name is probably a corruption of Cold Harbour. In an early Wren rebuild of 1672-8 some medieval walling was re-used for a plain rectangular building of six bays by three, with a north-west tower. It is faced in Portland stone. There are round-headed windows with bracketed cornices, balustraded parapets, and a curious leaded steeple rather as if an inverted hexagonal trumpet. The simple and spacious auditory interior has, unusually, a flat ceiling. Burnt out in 1941, the church, including the steeple, was reconstructed in 1961-2 by Arthur Bailey.

The setting of the church, here seen from the south west (right), has been much changed. The 'front' used to be to the north, but the making of Queen Victoria Street to the south in 1867-71, and clearance after wartime bombing, left the church somewhat high and dry. Keith New's 1962 east windows represent the extension of the Church overseas, with St Nicholas (above) as a figurehead on the ark (the Church).

The interior has also been transformed. A pre-war view (above) is dominated by ornament, notably the original reredos and Victorian glass. With many fittings gone, and pale-coloured woodwork, the space has become austere (right), essentially unembellished save for New's glass under remade swags. The pulpit is 17th century and the brass chandelier 18th century. The gilded statue of St Nicholas (left) was made in c. 1874 for a position over the gateway from Queen Victoria Street.

ST OLAVE HART STREET

◆

THIS SMALL medieval church is the City's best surviving example of the typical accretively built parish church from before 1666. The earliest parts to the west are of *c.* 1270 and include a crypt. Otherwise comprehensively rebuilt in the mid 15th century, the church has a three-bay nave and aisles, almost square, with a south-west tower. Every century since is represented: early 16th-century windows, a churchyard gateway and vestry from 1658-62, upper tower stages of 1731-2, and 19th-century repairs, including a mild restoration by Arthur Blomfield in 1871. Though the church was gutted by four strikes during the war, many fittings and a splendid collection of monuments have survived. In 1951-4 Ernest Glanfield restored the church, with sensitivity to its intimate character.

A view across the chancel steps (right) shows one of the Purbeck-marble quatrefoil arcade piers, probably from the 13th-century church and re-used in the 15th century. This stands amid later fittings — the pulpit of c. 1685, from Wren's St Benet Gracechurch Street (demolished 1867), and three of St Olave's four 18th-century sword-rests. The plasterwork angel (above) is from the ceiling of the 1661-2 vestry.

FROM St PAUL'S
CATHEDRAL
1934

S̲t Olave (left) is 'a country church in the world of Seething Lane' (John Betjeman). The walled churchyard is a remarkable survival in a fiercely commercial district. To the west, beyond medieval ragstone and Georgian brick, Gothic architecture's later life can be seen in Glanfield's bulky rectory of 1954, and the even bulkier Postmodern Minster Court. The churchyard gateway of 1658 (above), a rare survival, is taken from a 1633 design by the Dutch architect Hendrik de Keyser.

*T*he walls are festooned with monuments. The one to Sir James Deane (d. 1608), in the south aisle over the vestry door (left), shows him with his three wives, kneeling in prayer. The view looking east (above) shows the extent of renewal in the 1950s. The roofs, seating and reredos are all by Glanfield. The late 13th-century crypt (right), now a chapel, has a ribbed cross vault of Caen stone.

O lave, King of Norway, was martyred in 1030. His statue (left) was made in 1954 by Carl Schou, a Norwegian artist. Samuel Pepys, St Olave's most famous parishioner, had no memorial here until 1883, when a portrait in an aedicule (above) was made to designs by Blomfield. The 15th-century vestry doorway (right) retains its original door. The 1661-2 vestry has panelled walls as well as the plasterwork ceiling.

ST PETER CORNHILL

SITUATED ON the City's highest ground, and traditionally its oldest church foundation, St Peter does have ancient origins, perhaps dating from the Saxon re-occupation of the Roman forum. The church was rebuilt in 1677-84 by Wren and Hooke. They retained an aisled oblong medieval plan, re-using arcade-pier foundations, and rebuilt a south-west tower in brick, adding an obelisk spire. The church is largely concealed, surrounded by other buildings except to the east. The simple five-bay interior is little altered in form, with a tunnel-vaulted nave and transversely vaulted aisles. Though reseated, it has numerous good fittings. The church was restored in 1872 by J. D. Wyatt and in 1990 adapted to use by the Proclamation Trust as a Christian study centre.

The Woodmason monument of 1782 (above) commemorates seven children who died in a fire. Their father was at a ball at St James's Palace. The memorial is said to have been designed by Francesco Bartolozzi. The timber bell frame in the brick tower (right) appears to survive from the 17th century, with pegged construction and prominent carpenter's assembly marks.

The stuccoed east façade looking onto Gracechurch Street (left) is a nicely proportioned architectural display, its parapets swept up to a pediment in an Italian manner. Original woodwork (right) includes the west gallery, the carved doorcases below, the organ case by Father Smith and the pulpit with its tester. Victorian pews were removed in 1990. Martial glass in the aisles by Hugh Easton includes a window of 1960 (above) dedicated to the Royal Tank Regiment.

St Sepulchre without Newgate

St Sepulchre was the largest parish church in London before the Dissolution, and the largest post-Fire rebuilding. Standing outside the City walls, it was likened to the Holy Sepulchre in Jerusalem. The mid 15th-century three-storey south porch, paid for by Sir Hugh Popham, Chancellor of Normandy, is an important survival. It seems to antedate a rebuilding of *c.* 1470, the shell of which was retained in a 1667-71 reconstruction by the parish – to classical designs perhaps by the mason Joshua Marshall. Subsequent piecemeal alteration has added up to substantial re-Gothicization. The interior is 150 ft (45 m.) long and double aisled through eight bays, 'spacious and handsome, but less interesting than it might be' (B. F. L. Clarke). The church closed to regular worship in 1995.

The east window in the Royal Fusiliers' Chapel (above), by Gerald Smith, includes a vignette of the church. Ropes in the tower (right) are suggestive of the hangings that used to take place nearby. Newgate Prison's handbell, displayed in the church, was rung outside the cells of condemned prisoners before their execution. The ring of twelve bells is known as 'the bells of Old Bailey', after the nearby Court building.

The nave arcades (right), with monuments like barnacles on the columns, use the non-specific Tuscan/Doric Order characteristic of 17th-century churches in London before Wren. The coffered nave ceiling was made in 1834. Most of the woodwork is also 19th century. The 15th-century former Chapel of St Stephen has become the Musicians' Chapel (left). Its round-headed windows of 1789 within medieval arches contain mid 20th-century glass by Gerald Smith and Brian Thomas. Graffiti (above) is here an unorthodox method of keeping records.

From the south, Popham's porch is prominent (left). It was blandly refaced and given its oriel window by W. P. Griffith in 1873-5; original vaulting survives inside. The ragstone tower was rebuilt in 1630-4, but its features, including the absurdly outsized pinnacles, are principally due to Griffith. The Portland-stone south aisle was refenestrated and given buttresses by Arthur Billing in 1879-80. A 17th-century sundial survives in the parapet. Eighteenth-century Royal Arms (above), offset by standards, are situated over the south-aisle screen.

St Stephen Walbrook

ST STEPHEN is one of Wren's finest achievements, its interior a *tour de force*. It was the first domed church in Britain, and, in part, a dry run for St Paul's Cathedral. Built in 1672-80, it replaced a church of *c.* 1430 on Walbrook, a street made over a small tributary of the Thames.

A six-bay oblong with a longitudinal axis is combined and superbly resolved with a centralized plan in the form of a Greek Cross. This subtle Baroque ambivalence was achieved with little formal precedent save in much humbler cross-in-rectangle buildings. An elegant steeple was added in 1713-14.

The church was most recently restored in 1978-87 by Robert Potter, of Brandt Potter & Partners. The work included a controversial re-ordering, to a scheme devised and funded by Lord Palumbo.

*P**roportional sophistication is enhanced by lavish decoration. The coffered plasterwork of the lanterned wooden dome (above) is of the 1670s, reconstructed by Godfrey Allen in 1951-4 after war damage. In the west gallery, over Stuart Royal Arms, there is a fine 1765 Rococo organ case by G. P. England (right). The organ itself was replaced in 1888, and has since been much rebuilt.*

This is one of Wren's largest churches, but drama and spatial complexity fill the interior, giving the impression of a small space (left). Henry Moore's 1970s Travertine marble altarpiece is encircled by beechwood seating by Andrew Varah. The central altar reinforces the auditory centrality given by the dome, while the 1670s reredos is a reminder of the longitudinal emphasis of earlier liturgy. Externally the church is comparatively modest (right) and, with the dome, has a surprising Byzantine quality. Steps rise through a lobby (above), linking the street to the main interior.

215

St Vedast Foster Lane

A SIMPLE BUILDING, St Vedast is set apart by its unique Baroque spire. The medieval church, named after a 6th-century Frankish bishop, was perhaps founded by a Flemish community. The parish undertook the post-Fire rebuilding in 1669-72, but poorly; it had to be redone by Wren in 1695-99. Through all this, some medieval wall and an irregular shape were retained. From a double-aisled predecessor Wren fashioned a single-aisled interior, more suited to auditory worship, and moved the tower to the south west. The spire in the manner of Borromini was added in 1709-12, and is probably by Hawksmoor. The interior was gutted in 1940, and restored in 1953-63 by Stephen Dykes Bower, who created a serene space and introduced many attractive fittings.

The 1950s interior (right) has distinctive marble paving and collegiate seating, the Tuscan arcade to the south aisle concealed behind a screen. The reredos and communion rail are from St Christopher-le-Stocks (demolished 1781). The 1961 east-window glass depicting the life of St Vedast is by Brian Thomas and the lectern by Dykes Bower. The stunning aumbry (above) was made by Bernard Merry in 1992.

Seen from Cheapside (right), the lower parts of the stone church are humble, even clumsy, in their forms. This cannot be said of the dominant and architecturally subtly subversive spire with its intricate curved surfaces. The richly carved pulpit (left), from All Hallows Bread Street (demolished 1878), has some modern allegorical detail and elegantly swept stairs. The aedicular monument to Sir Edward Clark (d. 1705) is a typical piece of funerary carving (above); it too has symbolic elements.

A CITYSCAPE OF TOWERS

◆

THE 39 current or former Anglican parish churches make a
special contribution to the City of London townscape
(here St James Garlickhythe in front of St Paul's Cathedral). This is
also true of the City's handful of buildings erected for other forms
of religious worship. These diverse buildings range from the
12th- and 13th-century Royal Peculiar of the Temple Church of St
Mary, through the 1699-1701 Spanish and Portuguese Synagogue,
to the 1950-4 rebuilding of the Dutch Church, Austin Friars.

THE CITY TEMPLE

THE CITY TEMPLE was the second-largest Nonconformist chapel in London when it was built in 1873-4; only Spurgeon's Tabernacle in Southwark was bigger. The congregation traces its origins to 1640. The Victorian building, which cost the large sum of £35,000, was erected through the efforts of the minister Joseph Parker. Extensive basements were provided for schoolrooms, offices and the minister's house. The designs were by Lockwood & Mawson, Yorkshire architects, in a High Victorian eclectic classical style that is rare in London. Bombed in 1941, it was rebuilt between retained ends in 1955-8, to designs by Lord Mottistone, of Seely and Paget. Externally the rebuild has a concrete frame with stone wall panels. Inside there is a huge cinema-like hall.

The 1870s Bath-stone façade adjoins Holborn Viaduct (above). Its two-storey portico and three-stage tower with a cupola are in the manner of Wren, but with exotic elements. They seem strangely bolted on to the 1950s rebuild. Inside (right), where the pulpit dominates, there are thin cedar columns around the apse, with a round window by Hugh Easton.

THE DUTCH CHURCH AUSTIN FRIARS

◆

THE DUTCH CHURCH, wholly rebuilt in 1950-4, is a fine example of inventive classical church architecture, exceptional among the City's post-war churches for being uncomplicated by the presence of significant earlier fabric. The monastery church of the Augustine Friars was founded in 1253 and rebuilt after 1354. It was parcelled out after the Dissolution, the nave being given to Dutch and Flemish Protestants in 1550. In continuous use by the Dutch as 'Jesus Temple', the medieval church was destroyed by bombing in 1940. A substantially smaller building replaced it, to designs by Arthur Bailey. The church is above a meeting hall, the remainder of the site to the east being given over to an office block. Bailey's designs combine boldness and restraint, successfully synthesizing traditional and Modernist approaches.

From an array of striking stained glass by Max Nauta of Amsterdam come these figures of William and Mary (above), forming two lights of a window in the entrance lobby. A bright banner hangs in front of the Predikant's platform (right), before which stands the holy table. Fragments of the medieval stone altar can be seen in the floor.

The main interior (left) gives an impression of height and clarity of form that is characteristically Dutch. A sense of modernity is not undermined by the muted classicism of the coffered ceiling vault and fluted pilaster strips, nor by the traditional chandeliers. The Portland-stone exterior (above) is built up of block-like forms, neatly finished with a tall spirelet that is topped with a weathercock by John Skeaping. The relief carvings are by Esmond Burton.

*The tubular-steel-framed spiral staircase to the organ loft,
and the organ itself (above), combine the circular and the angular,
pointing up both the attention to detail in the design, and the excellent
finish of the craftsmanship. From the south wall (right) come the
Wilhelmina stained-glass window by D. Kok and a tapestry
representing the Achievements of Man by Hans van Norden.*

JEWIN WELSH CHURCH

◆

IN A RESIDENTIAL area where there are varied examples of first-class Modernist design, this Welsh Presbyterian chapel is in the style known in the 1950s as New Humanism, a non-doctrinaire English version of Modernism. It was built in 1960–61, to designs of 1956 by Caröe & Partners. The chapel is a simple brick rectangular hall, of structural interest for its concrete portal frame. There are copper roofs and a south-west tower. This building replaced a bomb-damaged chapel of 1878-9, by Charles Bell. This, in turn, was the successor to a chapel on Jewin Crescent, from which the name derives. That site is now within the Barbican estate. The congregation has its origins in a Welsh Calvinistic Methodist chapel founded in 1774 in Smithfield.

A general view of the interior (right) shows the pointed arches of the concrete frame. Tiered galleries form the traditional U-shape, these being continuous with the organ gallery behind the central pulpit. The woodwork, unpolished smoked American oak, is finished to a high standard. Several Eisteddfod chairs (above) have been given to the church.

St Etheldreda Ely Place

St Etheldreda is a rare example of an English medieval building in use for Roman Catholic worship. Its origins are as an adjunct to the town house of the bishops of Ely, an oratory of 1251 having been transformed into a private chapel in *c.* 1293. St Etheldreda was the 7th-century abbess who built a monastery on the site that became Ely Cathedral. In 1874 the building was acquired by the Fathers of the Institute of Charity, founded by the Abbate Rosmini. They restored the building in 1876-9, to designs by John Young and Bernard Whelan. Further works of restoration were carried out in 1935 and 1951. A small church, with only a gable end to the street, it has a cloistered garden and a luminous interior with much stained glass and interesting statuary.

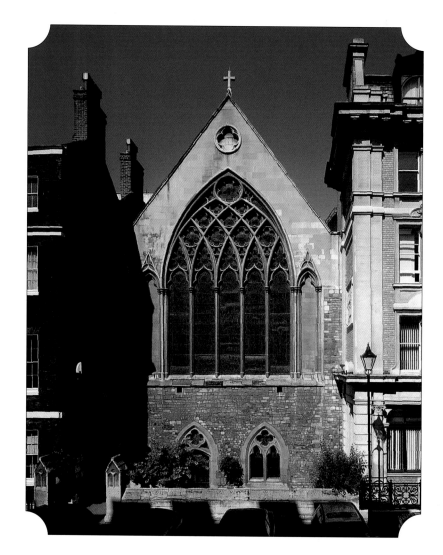

Ely Place is an orderly street of domestic character, dominated by 1770s brick terraces now converted into offices. The church comes as a surprise. Its east façade, of ragstone and ashlar (above), is slightly set back, as if not to draw too much attention to its disparities. The Stations of the Cross on the undercroft walls (right) are by May Blakeman, in reliefs said to be of carved polystyrene.

The remodelled main interior (right) has tall and narrow Gothic arcading along the north and south nave walls. Under crocketed gables between the windows there are painted statues, also by May Blakeman. These represent Roman Catholic martyrs of the Reformation. The glass in the east window is of 1951, by Joseph Nuttgens. Votive figures (above) stand in a niche in the Chapel of Our Lady.

The gable end walls have huge windows with elaborate c. 1293 tracery, 'the Geometrical just on the point of disintegrating into the illogicalities of the coming Dec[orated] style' (Nikolaus Pevsner). The stained glass of the west and north windows (above) is by Charles Blakeman. The undercroft of 1251 (left) has four-way timber bracing on moulded stone piers. These piers replaced decayed timber posts in the 1870s.

ST MARY MOORFIELDS

S<small>T</small> M<small>ARY</small> M<small>OORFIELDS</small>, the only purpose-built Roman Catholic church in the City, is the successor to an important building in English Catholic history from soon after the 1791 grant of freedom of worship. The present church was built in 1899-1903, with George Sherrin as architect. Externally discreet, its interior incorporates elements from its grander predecessor. This was built in 1817-20 in Moorfields, to Greek Revival designs by John Newman. For a time London's main Roman Catholic church, it had a dramatic *lumière mystérieuse* ensemble at its east end, based on that in the Church of St Sulpice in Paris – its huge theatrical fresco of the Crucifixion, by Agostino Aglio is now lost. Its relatively modest successor has fittings by J. Daymond & Son.

The apsidal sanctuary (right) has paired fluted Corinthian columns from Charles Parker's 1852 refitting of the 1817-20 building. Parker replaced a Tuscan screen designed by Giovanni Battista Comelli (of Milan) that stood in front of Aglio's Crucifixion. The c. 1820 marble sarcophagus altar is by Comelli. A relief panel comes from a Stations of the Cross series (above).

*T*he Portland-stone façade to Eldon Street (right) does not appear to be that of a church. Functional shop fronts and upper storeys (which house the presbytery) suggest the commercial use that is to be expected in this district. However, the elaborate arched portal with the Virgin and Child in a segmental pediment, and the carved relief frieze panels on either side depicting scenes from the Life of Mary, do indicate what lies behind. The sculpture is by Daymond & Son.

*T*he humble four-bay interior (above) has a vaulted nave and a single aisle, with Devonshire marble columns and pilasters to Tuscan arcading. A mosaic lunette (right) depicts the beheading of Sir Thomas More on Tower Hill. It is positioned over the marble entrance to a north-west chapel which is dedicated to More, the scholar and statesman, author of Utopia (1516), and opponent of the English Reformation.

THE SPANISH AND PORTUGUESE SYNAGOGUE

THIS IS THE oldest surviving English synagogue and therefore of exceptional historic importance. It is also a delightful building, scarcely altered since it was built for Sephardic worship in 1699–1701. Under the Commonwealth, Jews were permitted to settle in England for the first time since their expulsion in 1290. The first 'resettlement' synagogue was built for Iberian Jews in 1657 in Creechurch Lane. The present building, off the street called Bevis Marks, was its replacement. Built, and perhaps designed, by Joseph Avis, a Quaker carpenter, it has much in common with Christian chapels of the period. It is a simple red-brick box with a galleried interior. This interior is a glorious space, opulently fitted with fine woodwork and low-slung brass chandeliers.

There are seven chandeliers (above), representing the days of the week. At the east end the Echal around the Ark (right), wherein the Torah scrolls are kept, resembles a contemporary Christian reredos. In the upper stage the Decalogue (Ten Commandments) in Hebrew is as originally painted. On the Ark rails are some of the ten brass candlesticks that correspond to the Ten Commandments.

The interior (above) is a simple oblong under a flat ceiling, with Tuscan columns supporting lattice-fronted galleries around three sides. Open-backed benches doubling as chests for prayer books and shawls face inwards to accord with Sephardic ritual. Towards the west end is the Bimah, or railed reading platform, in front of which sits the Rabbi. Against the north wall is a canopied choir stall of c. 1850.

*J*ews were forbidden to build in a high street, so the synagogue is behind a small courtyard. Its external appearance (left) does not proclaim its function. The simple brick elevations have two tiers of windows separated by a stone band. There is a lamp on a big horizontal iron bracket in front of the pedimented west entrance. The wealth of good furniture includes a circumcision chair (above) of c. 1790, in Sheraton style; Benjamin Disraeli was among those to have been circumcised here.

THE TEMPLE CHURCH

❖

THE TEMPLE CHURCH of St Mary is at the heart of the quiet lawyers' haven that is the Middle and Inner Temple. It is a medieval building of international importance, yet relatively little known. Comprising two distinct sections, both architecturally notable, it has a round nave of *c.* 1160-85 and a 'hall' chancel of *c.* 1220-40. The rare circular form of the nave was favoured by the Templars (an order of military monks linked to the Crusades), in imitation of the Holy Sepulchre in Jerusalem. Consecrated by Patriarch Heraclius of Jerusalem, this nave is one of England's earliest Gothic buildings. The chancel is an exemplary work in the more resolved Gothic style of 50 years later. The church is also renowned for its 13th-century effigies of Knights who supported the Templars. The building's foremost qualities have been maintained through extensive restoration, in the period 1825 to 1862, and in 1947-57 by Walter H. Godfrey, following severe war damage.

The only effigy of a Knight to have survived intact (above) is identified as that of Robert de Ros (d. 1227). He has military accoutrements and a shield of arms with water bottles. The Bath-stone exterior (right) was largely refaced in the 19th century. The parapets to the round nave have been restored since; the crenellation may originally have been meant to reflect the military character of the Templars.

The restored interior from within the round nave (left) appears uniformly Gothic. However, the 12th-century nave is 'Transitional' in style, with intersecting round-arched (Norman) arcading to the triforium. The 13th-century chancel beyond, five bays with aisles as tall as the nave, is pure early Gothic, 'airy, yet sturdy, generous in all its spacing, but disciplined and sharply pulled together' (Nikolaus Pevsner). In the chancel is a Purbeck-marble effigy (above), probably of Bishop Sylvester of Carlisle (d. 1255), with fine stiff-leaf carving on the crook.

A view of the church from before 1940 and its most recent restoration, shows it surrounded by dignified blocks of legal chambers (above). The estate established by the Templars was taken by the Crown after the order was suppressed in 1312, and soon after it was occupied by lawyers. The church, which remains a Royal Peculiar, was later presented to the Law Societies. The Purbeck-marble effigies in the nave floor (left) were badly damaged in 1941.

*T*he round nave (left) is 59 ft (18 m.) across. It has a rib-vaulted ambulatory with blank arcading backing a continuous bench. Purbeck-marble quatrefoil piers with waterleaf capitals give rise to slender shafts ascending to the triforium and the clerestory. All the Purbeck marble was renewed in the 1947-57 restoration. An elaborate heraldic floor brass (above) commemorates Edward Littleton (d. 1664).

Stepped triple lancet windows in the chancel are elegantly moulded. Those to the east (left) hold superb stained glass of 1957-8 by Carl Edwards. The post-war restoration enlarged the nave triforium (above). Post-Reformation monuments had been deposited here in 1840, and commemoration of the dead remains its purpose. Encaustic tiles of 1842 by Thomas Willement have been moved to the triforium floor. A detail (right) represents the Agnus Dei (Lamb of God).

APPENDIX

———◆———

THE ROYAL COMMISSION ON THE HISTORICAL MONUMENTS OF ENGLAND

The Royal Commission on the Historical Monuments of England is responsible for compiling the national record of England's historic buildings and archaeological sites. The records produced in our surveys are available to the public through the National Monuments Record, the RCHME's public archive, which contains over 7 million items, including important collections of historic photography. The RCHME also publishes books which present its work to the public.

The approximately 2,000 photographs that make up the 1995 City Churches survey are open to public view in the London Search Room of the National Monuments Record (55 Blandford Street, London W1H 3AF, tel: 0171 208 8200, fax: 0171 224 5333). The City Churches survey was part-funded by the Corporation of London, and prints of the photographs can also be seen at the Corporation's Guildhall Library (Aldermanbury, London EC2P 2EJ, tel: 0171 606 3030, fax: 0171 600 3384). Both of these archives also hold extensive earlier records relating to the City Churches, notably many photographs which show us how the buildings looked at earlier dates.

The National Monuments Record is held at the National Monuments Record Centre, Swindon (Kemble Drive, Swindon SN2 2GZ, tel: 01793 414700, fax: 01793 414707), and covers buildings outside London, as well as archaeological sites, maritime sites and air photographs for the whole of England. The building is also the RCHME's headquarters.

National Monuments Record Buildings Index File Numbers for the City Churches Survey

All Hallows Barking by the Tower	94258
All Hallows London Wall	94259
St Andrew Holborn	94261
St Andrew Undershaft	94262
St Andrew by the Wardrobe	94260
St Anne and St Agnes	94263
St Bartholomew the Great	94264
St Bartholomew the Less	94265
St Benet Paul's Wharf	94266
St Botolph without Aldersgate	78493
St Botolph Aldgate	94267
St Botolph Bishopsgate	94268
St Bride Fleet Street	94269
St Clement Eastcheap	94270
St Dunstan in the West	94271
St Edmund King and Martyr	94272
St Ethelburga Bishopsgate	78980
St Giles Cripplegate	94273
St Helen Bishopsgate	94274
St James Garlickhythe	94275
St Katherine Cree	93019
St Lawrence Jewry	94276
St Magnus the Martyr	94277
St Margaret Lothbury	94278
St Margaret Pattens	94279
St Martin Ludgate	94280
St Mary Abchurch	94281
St Mary Aldermary	93255
St Mary le Bow	94283
St Mary at Hill	87965
St Mary Woolnoth	94284
St Michael Cornhill	94285
St Michael Paternoster Royal	94286
St Nicholas Cole Abbey	54962
St Olave Hart Street	94287
St Peter Cornhill	94288
St Sepulchre without Newgate	94289
St Stephen Walbrook	94290
St Vedast Foster Lane	94291
The City Temple	94292
The Dutch Church Austin Friars	94293
Jewin Welsh Church	77329
St Etheldreda Ely Place	94296
St Mary Moorfields	94297
The Spanish and Portuguese Synagogue	94294
The Temple Church	94295

PHOTOGRAPHS ILLUSTRATED

◆

RCHME NEGATIVE NUMBERS

p. 3	BB97/7246	p. 65	BB95/14941	p. 114	BB95/16572	p. 163	BB95/11739	p. 212	BB95/11852
p. 9	BB95/980		BB95/14945	p. 115	BB94/11501	p. 164	BB95/11778	p. 213	BB95/11851
p. 14	BB95/11818		BB95/14936		BB94/11476	p. 165	AA63/1323	p. 214	BB95/11840
p. 16	BB95/3954	p. 66	BB95/13224	p. 116	BB95/8901		BB95/11740	p. 215	BB95/11837
p. 17	BB95/3923	p. 67	BB97/5232	p. 117	BB95/8919	p. 166	BB95/11762		BB95/14903
p. 18	BB95/3956	p. 68	BB95/13206	p. 118	BB91/20019		AA61/2726	p. 216	BB95/13490
p. 19	BB95/13411		BB95/13217		BB95/8903	p. 167	BB95/11772	p. 217	BB95/13467
p. 20	BB95/3919	p. 69	BB95/13208	p. 119	BB95/8899		BB73/5594	p. 218	BB95/13475
p. 21	BB95/3949		BB95/13214	p. 120	BB95/4039	p. 168	BB95/11743		BB95/13494
	BB95/3961	p. 70	BB95/11631	p. 121	BB95/4030	p. 169	BB95/11732		BB95/13461
p. 22	BB95/3944	p. 71	BB95/11614	p. 122	BB95/4021	p. 170	BB95/14730	p. 219	BB95/13461
	BB95/3983	p. 72	BB95/11616	p. 123	BB95/4048	p. 171	BB95/14709	p. 220-221	FF97/85
p. 23	BB95/3985		BB95/11610		BB95/4042	p. 172	BB97/5235	p. 222	BB95/10349
p. 24	BB95/8984	p. 73	BB95/11600	p. 124	BB95/9981		BB95/14731	p. 223	BB95/10357
p. 25	BB95/8974	p. 74	BB95/9189	p. 125	BB95/9967	p. 173	BB95/14721	p. 224	BB95/11525
p. 26	BB95/8952	p. 75	BB95/9161	p. 126	BB95/9973	p. 174	BB95/5828	p. 225	BB95/11498
p. 27	BB95/8956	p. 76	BB95/14836		BB95/9956	p. 175	BB95/14755	p. 226	BB95/11490
	BB95/8953	p. 77	BB95/14831	p. 127	BB95/9963	p. 176	BB95/5819	p. 227	BB95/11485
p. 28	BB95/3895	p. 78	BB95/9182	p. 128	BB95/10387	p. 177	BB95/5839	p. 228	BB95/11499
p. 29	BB95/14748		BB95/9167	p. 129	BB95/10368	p. 178	BB95/14754	p. 229	BB95/11517
p. 30	BB95/3852	p. 79	BB95/9191	p. 130	BB95/10363	p. 179	BB95/5840		BB95/11501
	BB46/923	p. 80	BB95/14808	p. 131	BB95/10370		BB95/5836	p. 230	BB91/18265
p. 31	BB95/3864	p. 81	BB95/6087	p. 132	BB95/10374	p. 180	BB95/14635	p. 231	BB91/18258
p. 32	BB95/3877	p. 82	AA61/2659		BB95/10372	p. 181	BB95/14602	p. 232	BB95/9905
p. 33	BB95/3879		BB69/2583	p. 133	BB95/10377	p. 182	BB95/14593	p. 233	BB95/9940
p. 34	BB95/5902	p. 83	BB95/14802	p. 134	BB95/13192	p. 183	BB95/14625	p. 234	BB95/9912
p. 35	BB95/5882	p. 84	BB95/6085	p. 135	BB95/13174		BB95/14609		BB95/9927
p. 36	BB95/5885	p. 85	BB95/6102	p. 136	BB95/14785	p. 184	BB95/14616	p. 235	BB95/9923
	BB95/5913	p. 86	BB95/6106	p. 137	BB95/13168	p. 185	BB95/14595		BB95/9931
p. 37	BB95/5891	p. 87	BB95/6103		BB95/13176	p. 186	BB95/10011	p. 236	BB95/13506
p. 38	BB95/9032	p. 88	BB95/10332	p. 138	BB95/13177	p. 187	BB95/10015	p. 237	BB95/13380
p. 39	BB95/9006	p. 89	BB95/10326	p. 139	BB95/13180	p. 188	BB95/9996	p. 238	BB95/13371
p. 40	BB95/9038	p. 90	BB95/13251	p. 140	BB95/13533	p. 189	BB95/10009	p. 239	BB95/13377
	BB95/9008	p. 91	BB95/13241	p. 141	BB95/13557		BB95/9986		BB95/13505
p. 41	BB95/14778	p. 92	BB95/13243	p. 142	BB95/14573	p. 190	BB95/6027	p. 240	BB95/11797
p. 42	BB95/4184	p. 93	BB95/13245		BB46/1231	p. 191	BB95/6000	p. 241	BB95/11789
p. 43	BB95/4176		BB95/13265	p. 143	BB95/13555	p. 192	AA61/2741	p. 242	BB95/11787
p. 44	BB95/4149	p. 94	BB95/13232		BB95/14566		BB95/6022	p. 243	BB95/11780
p. 45	BB95/4155	p. 95	BB95/14795	p. 144	BB95/14677	p. 193	BB95/6007		BB95/11790
p. 46	BB95/4189	p. 96	BB95/13227	p. 145	BB95/14706	p. 194	BB95/13144	p. 244	BB95/10065
	BB95/4157		BB95/13262	p. 146	BB95/14650	p. 195	BB95/13138	p. 245	BB95/14822
p. 47	BB95/4194	p. 97	BB95/13302	p. 147	BB95/14646	p. 196	BB95/13121	p. 246	BB95/10032
p. 48	BB95/961	p. 98	BB95/6072	p. 148	BB95/14696	p. 197	BB95/13123		BB95/10063
p. 49	BB95/970	p. 99	BB95/6065	p. 149	BB95/14672	p. 198	BB95/13139	p. 247	CC66-430
p. 50	BB95/14882	p. 100	BB95/6040		BB95/14680	p. 199	BB95/13131		BB82/11294
p. 51	BB95/974		BB95/6059	p. 150	BB95/13533		BB95/13148	p. 248	BB95/10034
p. 52	BB95/983	p. 101	BB95/6033	p. 151	BB95/13519	p. 200	BB95/13146	p. 249	BB95/10059
p. 53	BB95/1058	p. 102	BB95/14783	p. 152	BB95/13523		BB95/13149	p. 250	BB95/10089
p. 54	BB95/1019	p. 103	BL 24752		BB95/13516	p. 201	BB95/13141	p. 251	BB95/10039
p. 55	BB95/1002	p. 104	BB95/9136	p. 153	BB95/13509	p. 202	BB95/5867		BB95/10041
	BB95/1027	p. 105	BB95/9125	p. 154	BB95/13547	p. 203	BB95/5871		
p. 56	BB95/13438	p. 106	CC56/62	p. 155	BB95/13535	p. 204	BB95/14757	FRONT COVER:	
p. 57	BB95/13423	p. 107	CC56/14760		BB95/13537	p. 205	BB95/5880	BB95/11739	
p. 58	BB95/13441	p. 108	BB95/9140	p. 156	BB95/11813		BB95/5847		
p. 59	BB95/13431		BB95/9104	p. 157	BB95/14896	p. 206	BB95/798	BACK COVER (CLOCKWISE):	
	BB95/13454	p. 109	BB95/9117	p. 158	BB95/11801	p. 207	BB95/767	BB95/3923	
p. 60	BB95/14935	p. 110	BB95/16592	p. 159	BB95/11805	p. 208	BB95/822	BB95/4176	
p. 61	BB95/14914	p. 111	BB94/11495	p. 160	BB95/11832		BB95/772	BB95/11741	
p. 62	BB95/14948	p. 112	CC73/2057	p. 161	BB64/548	p. 209	BB95/730	BB95/11797	
p. 63	BB95/14923	p. 113	BB95/16587		BB95/11810	p. 210	BB95/13397		
p. 64	BB95/14926		BB95/16589	p. 162	BB95/11760	p. 211	BB95/740		

253

SELECT BIBLIOGRAPHY

This is a short list of some major published sources that cover the City Churches as a group of buildings. It does not include guidebooks and other publications on particular churches, of which there are many; nor does it include early or more obscure publications that would be more difficult to locate. In the preparation of the text for this book two sources were particularly valuable, Simon Bradley's revision of Nikolaus Pevsner's text for the latest edition of the *Buildings of England* volume relating to the City of London and Paul Jeffery's *The City Churches of Sir Christopher Wren*. Any mistakes, however, are our own.

C. Amery, *Wren's London* (Luton, 1988).

J. Betjeman, *The City of London Churches* (London, 1974).

G. H. Birch, *London Churches of the 17th and 18th Centuries* (London, 1896).

S. Bradley and N. Pevsner, *The Buildings of England: London 1: The City of London* (London, 1997).

B. F. L. Clarke, *Parish Churches of London* (London, 1966).

G. Cobb, *The Old Churches of London* (3 edns, London 1941-8), revised as *London City Churches* (London, 1977).

K. Downes, *The Architecture of Wren* (London, 1982).

G. Huelin, *Vanished Churches of the City of London* (London, 1996).

A. H. Mackmurdo, *Wren's City Churches* (Orpington, 1883).

P. Jeffery, *The City Churches of Sir Christopher Wren* (London, 1996).

S. Porter, *The Great Fire of London* (Stroud, 1996).

Royal Commission on Historical Monuments, *London,* iv, *The City* (London, 1929).

J. Schofield *et al*, 'Saxon and Medieval Parish Churches in the City of London: A Review', in *Transactions of the London and Middlesex Archaeological Society*, xlv (London, 1994), pp. 23-145.

M. Whinney, *Wren* (London, 1971).

The Wren Society, ix and x (Oxford, 1932-3).

E. and W. Young, *London's Churches* (London, 1986).

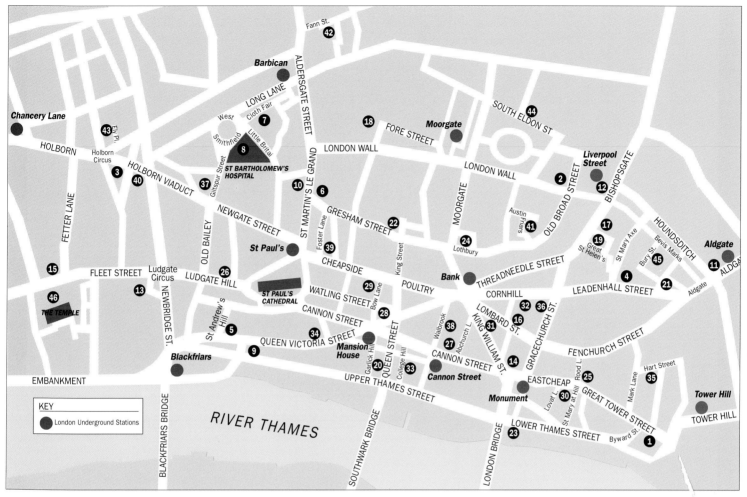

Where to find the City Churches

1 All Hallows Barking by the Tower
2 All Hallows London Wall
3 St Andrew Holborn
4 St Andrew Undershaft
5 St Andrew by the Wardrobe
6 St Anne and St Agnes
7 St Bartholomew the Great
8 St Bartholomew the Less
9 St Benet Paul's Wharf
10 St Botolph without Aldersgate
11 St Botolph Aldgate
12 St Botolph Bishopsgate
13 St Bride Fleet Street
14 St Clement Eastcheap
15 St Dunstan in the West
16 St Edmund King and Martyr
17 St Ethelburga Bishopsgate

18 St Giles Cripplegate
19 St Helen Bishopsgate
20 St James Garlickhythe
21 St Katherine Cree
22 St Lawrence Jewry
23 St Magnus the Martyr
24 St Margaret Lothbury
25 St Margaret Pattens
26 St Martin Ludgate
27 St Mary Abchurch
28 St Mary Aldermary
29 St Mary le Bow
30 St Mary at Hill
31 St Mary Woolnoth
32 St Michael Cornhill
33 St Michael Paternoster
   Royal

34 St Nicholas Cole Abbey
35 St Olave Hart Street
36 St Peter Cornhill
37 St Sepulchre without Newgate
38 St Stephen Walbrook
39 St Vedast Foster Lane
40 The City Temple
41 The Dutch Church Austin Friars

42 Jewin Welsh Church
43 St Etheldreda Ely Place
44 St Mary Moorfields
45 The Spanish and Portuguese
   Synagogue
46 The Temple Church

Information on Access to the City Churches
The Friends of the City Churches, 68 Battersea High Street, London SW11 3HX (tel: 0171 228 3336, fax: 0171 223 2714), keep up-to-date information on the opening times of the City Churches. In addition a free guide booklet, *City of London Churches*, published by Richard C. Martin with the Southwark Heritage Association in 1996, includes times of opening as then current. It may be available in the churches, at the Guildhall Library, or at tourist information centres.

INDEX

◆

OF ARCHITECTS, ARTISTS AND CRAFTSMEN

Aglio, Agostino 236
Alexandrescu, Petre 90
Allen, Godfrey 12, 80, 104, 108, 150, 212
Avis, Joseph 240
Ayres, Arthur 38

Babic, Petre and Mihai 90
Bailey, Arthur 12, 190, 224
Banks, Thomas 134
Barnes, John 170
Bartolozzi, Francesco 202
Bell, Charles, 230
Bentley, John Francis 11, 70, 72
Betts, Lukyn 24
Biggs, Peter 128
Billing, Arthur 211
Blacker, Thetis 72
Blakeman, Charles 235
Blakeman, May 232, 234
Blomfield, Arthur 194, 200
Blyth, J. 66
Bodley and Garner 134
Borley, J. H. 27
Braddock & Martin-Smith 42
Brandt Potter & Partners 212
Brown, Cecil 12, 124, 127
Brown, Robert 36
Burton, Esmond 227
Butterfield, William 88, 174, 177

Cachemaille-Day, N. F. 74
Caröe and Partners 230
Caröe and Passmore 98
Chamberlin, Powell & Bon 106
Champneys, Basil 88
Cheltenham, Mr 42
Christian, Ewan 147
Clarke, T. Chatfeild 34
Clarkson, Nathaniel 66
Clayton (John) and Bell (Alfred) 11, 180
Clutterbuck, Charles 72
Comelli, Giovanni Battista 236
Comper, Ninian 88, 102
Compton (John) Company 85
The Conservation Practice 170
Cooper, Paul A. 38

Dance, George (the Elder) 11, 70, 73-4
Dance, George (the Younger) 11, 24, 27, 56, 66, 128
Dance, Giles 74
Davies, Elidir 186
Daymond (J.) & Son 236, 238
Della Robbia 143
Dickinson, William 10, 156, 183
Dykes Bower, Stephen 12, 216

Easton, Hugh 59, 205, 222
Edwards, Carl 251
England, G. P. 212

Faithcraft 169
Foster, Peter 38

Gale, Alexander 116
Gardner, Starkie 55
Gibbons, Grinling 11, 16, 124, 137, 150
Glanfield, Ernest 194, 197, 199
Glasby, William 74
Godfrey, Walter H. 244
Gould, James 11, 74
Goulden, Richard 184
Griffith, J. William 68
Griffith, W. P. 211

Hardwick, P. C. 56, 59
Hardwick, Thomas 11, 56
Harris, Renatus 21
Harris, Thomas 95
Harrison and Harrison 21
Hawksmoor, Nicholas 8, 10, 11, 28, 80, 98, 100, 118, 174, 179, 183, 186, 216
Hayward, John 12, 166, 186
Heaton, Butler and Bayne 11, 36, 180
Hooke, Robert 10, 38, 42, 60, 98, 100, 124, 136, 144, 202

Ingram, W. Rowlands 138
Innes, Charles 156

Jones, Glyn 80

Kempe (C. E.) and Company 93
de Keyser, Hendrik 197
King, Lawrence 12, 162, 166
Kingsfield, Christopher 70
Kok, D. 228

Lester and Pack 24
Lockwood & Mawson 222

Mander, Noel 124, 189
Marshall, Joshua 206
Mears and Stainbank 40, 108
Meredith, Michael 74
Merry, Bernard 216
Moore, Henry 12, 215
Mottistone (Lord) 16, 222
    see also Seely and Paget

Nauta, Max 224
New, Keith 190, 192
Newman, John 236
Newton, I. H. 27
Nicholson (A. K.) Studios 108
van Norden, Hans 228
Nuttgens, Joseph 234
Nye, David 24

Oliver, John 10

Parker, Charles 236
Pearson, James 66
Pearson, J. L. 112-3
Philip, John Birnie 180, 184
Potter, Robert 212
Powell (James) & Sons 149

Rogers, William Gibbs 11, 170, 180, 184
Royal Electrical and Military Engineers 127

Savage, James 172
Schou, Carl 200
Scott, George Gilbert 11
Seely and Paget 12, 16, 28, 30, 56
Shaw, John (the Elder) 11, 90
Shaw, John (the Younger) 90
Sherrin, George 236

Sisson, Marshall 12, 38
Skeaping, John 227
Smith, David Lockhart 116
Smith, F. W. 134
Smith, Father 116, 123, 205
Smith, Gerald 206, 208
Snow, William 152
Stephenson, Kevin 74
Streeter, Robert 183
Strong, Edward 124

Tapper, Walter 13, 134
Tatchell, Rodney 70, 98
Taylor (John) and Company 86
Terry, Quinlan 12, 110
Thomas, Brian 12, 30, 33, 208, 216
Tijou, Jean 36
Travers, Martin 128, 132
Tress, Richard 156

Varah, Andrew 215

Webb, Aston 11, 48, 50, 52
Webb, Christopher and John 124
Webb, John 60
Weeks, Sister Catherine 138
Whelan, Bernard 232
Willement, Thomas 95, 251
Woodroffe, Edward 10
Wren, Christopher 8, 10-15, 28, 30, 38, 42, 60, 62, 73, 76, 80, 88, 100, 116, 120, 124, 128, 130, 134, 137, 140, 142, 150, 156, 162, 165, 167, 169-70, 186, 190, 194, 202, 208, 212, 215-16, 222
Wright, Nathaniel 11, 66
Wyatt, J. D. 202

Young, John 232

L   O   N